DANIEL

DANIEL
MAKING THE RIGHT CHOICES

EDWARD G. DOBSON

Fleming H. Revell
A Division of Baker Book House Co
Grand Rapids, Michigan 49516

Published by Fleming H. Revell
a division of Baker Book House Company
P.O. Box 6287, Grand Rapids, MI 49516-6287

Printed in the United States of America

Library of Congress Cataloging-in-Publication Data

Dobson, Ed.
   Daniel : making the right choices / Edward G. Dobson.
     p. cm.
   ISBN 0-8007-5529-4
   1. Bible. O.T. Daniel—Commentaries. I. Title.
BS1555.3.D64 1994
224'.507—dc20
                                   94-17141

Contents

Part 1

The Life of Daniel

Introduction

When I was growing up in Belfast, Northern Ireland, I heard many sermons from the Book of Daniel. I remember Sunday nights when the hall was so crowded that I sat with my friends on the steps of the pulpit so adults could have a seat. I remember nights when people lined up for a block down the street in order to get in. They were exciting services. I heard about the four beasts, the lion with eagle wings, the bear, the leopard, and the dreadful beast. I heard about Antichrist along with suggestions as to who he might be. I heard about the ram and the goat, the little horn and Antiochus. I heard detailed explanations about the seventieth week and how we were living in the last days. The preachers were convinced that Antichrist was alive, the Roman Empire ready to reemerge, and Christ about to return. All of that was over thirty years ago.

What I do *not* remember is any teaching on Daniel as a person living in a pagan culture. The entire focus was the apocalyptic section of Daniel's book, namely chapters 7–12. However, the first six chapters deal with Daniel and the pressures he encountered in maintaining his commitment to God in a foreign country. His story is in the trenches of everyday life.

I know that when I preach, some people think, "Ah, that's nice preachin', Dobson, but you don't understand the real world. You sit in your study surrounded by books. You live in a Christian environment. You don't understand where I am living." They are absolutely correct. I don't understand the ethical issues people struggle with every day. I don't understand the pressures of maintaining integrity in a world that rejects God. But the Book of Daniel is the story of a person who does understand. He faced those struggles. He was confronted with difficult and painful choices, and it all began when he was a young adult. He was somewhere between the ages of fourteen and nineteen when we pick up the story in Daniel 1. He had been taken from his family, his religious environment, and his support group. He was taken to a foreign country where he was asked to be part of a culture that pressured him to reject his religious roots. Here is a story that offers hope and insight for believers who live and work in environments where they are a minority.

Part one of this book (chapters 1–10) deals with the life of Daniel. Daniel was not a prophet, a priest, or a king. He was a politician and a civil servant. He served God in a thoroughly pagan government, and yet he remained true to God. The first part of this book is a practical manual on how to stay true to God in the secular marketplace.

The second part (chapters 11–17) deals with the prophetic section of the Book of Daniel and examines the three basic viewpoints concerning future events and Christ's return.

Chapter One

When Your World Falls Apart

Daniel 1:1–7

We all like to be in control of our circumstances. It gives us a sense of stability and security. When our family is watching television, I like to hold the remote control. Then I can change the channels when I want to. It drives me crazy when one of the kids flips channels instead of me. Life is the same way. As long as we have the remote control, everything is okay. But when God starts flipping channels, then life can be challenging. We feel we have lost control.

Losing Control

In the third year of the reign of Jehoiakim king of Judah, Nebuchadnezzar king of Babylon came to Jerusalem and besieged it. And the Lord delivered Jehoiakim king of Judah into his hand, along with some of the articles from the temple of God. These he carried off to the temple of his god in Babylonia and put in the treasure house of his god.

Daniel 1:1–2

About 650 years before the birth of Christ, the ancient world was ruled by the Assyrians (modern-day Syria). After 650 B.C., the power of the

Assyrians began a decline that continued for the rest of that century. At the time of this decline, a new world power was in the formative stages and would eventually dominate the world. This power was located in modern-day Iraq and was called the Chaldean or Babylonian Empire. Assyria (in the north) is in decline, and Babylon (in the south) is on the rise.

Meanwhile, in Egypt, Pharaoh Neco decides he has had enough of Syrian domination and the advance of the Babylonian armies. He decides to confront the Syrian armies by marching north through Israel. King Josiah of Israel decides to fight the Egyptian armies, and he is defeated and killed. Pharaoh Neco places Josiah's son Jehoiakim on the throne of Israel as a puppet king. Jehoiakim is forced to pay excessive taxes to Egypt.

Pharaoh Neco then decides to march north to defeat the Assyrian army and then march south to defeat the Babylonian armies. If he can accomplish this, then Egypt will rule the ancient world. But he is defeated by Nebuchadnezzar, the military leader of the Babylonian armies. Nebuchadnezzar then marches on to Jerusalem and surrounds it. During the siege, Nebuchadnezzar's father Nabopolassar (who is the king of Babylon) dies, and Nebuchadnezzar is called back to Babylon and anointed king of this new empire.

> And the Lord delivered Jehoiakim king of Judah into his hand, along with some of the articles from the temple of God. These he carried off to the temple of his god in Babylonia and put in the treasure house of his god.
>
> Daniel 1:2

One thing is for sure, the people of Israel are no longer in control of their land, their city, their lives, and their future. Even bad experiences come from God.

This is a humiliating time in Jewish history.

1. Jerusalem is overtaken by the Babylonians.
2. The king is taken captive.
3. The sacred vessels are removed from the temple.
4. The sacred vessels are placed in the pagan temple in Babylon.
5. The future leadership is taken to Babylon.

To be dominated by a foreign power was a disgrace. To lose the sacred vessels of the temple was a tragedy. To have these vessels placed in the temple of Baal was blasphemy. Yet in all of these tragedies there is a divine perspective: "And the *Lord delivered* Jehoiakim king of Judah into his hand, along with some of the articles from the temple of God" (v. 2, italics added). The divine reality is that God engineered *all* of these tragedies for his own purpose.

Why did God allow it? Fortunately, we do have the answer to that question. The answer is found in the writings of Isaiah, a prophet who lived and ministered during these troubled times in Israel. In fact, he predicted that all of this would happen.

> See, the LORD is going to lay
> waste the earth
> and devastate it;
> he will ruin its face
> and scatter its inhabitants—
> it will be the same
> for priest as for people,
> for master as for servant,
> for mistress as for maid,
> for seller as for buyer,
> for borrower as for lender,
> for debtor as for creditor.
> The earth will be completely laid
> waste
> and totally plundered.
> The LORD has spoken
> this word.
> The earth dries up and withers,
> the world languishes and
> withers,
> the exalted of the earth
> languish.
> The earth is defiled by its people;
> they have disobeyed the laws,
> violated the statutes
> and broken the everlasting
> covenant.
> Isaiah 24:1–5

Isaiah issues a message of warning. God is going to destroy the land. No one will escape. Creditor, debtor, borrower, lender, priest, people. No one will escape the judgment of God. Why will God bring about this judgment and desolation? Because his people have defiled themselves. They have broken his laws; they have violated his commandments. They have turned their back on his covenant.

When in Rome, Do As the Romans

The king ordered Ashpenaz, chief of his court officials, to bring in some of the Israelites from the royal family and the nobility.

Daniel 1:3

The Babylonians had a unique political strategy. When they conquered a foreign country, they collected the brightest young minds in that country. They would bring them to Babylon and retrain them, instructing them in the language, culture, law, and religion of the Babylonians. Then they would place these people back in their home country to rule it in behalf of the Babylonians.

The Babylonians demanded an impressive resume before they would put people in their training program. The prerequisites included the following (v. 4):

1. young,
2. no physical defect,
3. handsome,
4. aptitude for every kind of learning,
5. well informed,
6. quick to understand,
7. qualified to serve in the palace.

The Babylonians had a carefully developed strategy for training these potential leaders:

1. *Change their language.* The first step was to teach them the Babylonian language (v. 4). To be accepted in a new culture and to better understand that culture, it is imperative to learn their language. I remember in 1964 when our family emigrated to the United States from Northern Ireland. Even though both countries speak English, there is a vast differ-

ence in word usage, slang, and accent. I was fourteen at the time and was placed in eleventh grade. My worst memories were between classes when girls would gather around me in the hall and say, "Talk for us!" They liked my accent, but I was embarrassed, and I determined those first few months in America that I would learn an American accent so that I would not stand out as different.

2. *Change their literature.* The second step was to introduce these potential leaders to the vast array of Babylonian literature. The literature of a culture is really a window into how that culture perceives itself and the larger world. It is also a window into its values. In my last year of high school I took a course on American history. In Ireland I had studied the American Revolution from a British viewpoint. The British spin was that they were too busy in India to worry about America and had they really desired to defeat America they would have. This was not exactly the perspective I learned from an American teacher in an American classroom teaching from an American book. The American spin was a lot different. The Americans believed that they broke the back of all the power of the British Empire!

3. *Change their lifestyle.* The third step was to introduce the best of Babylonian food. "The king assigned them a daily amount of food and wine from the king's table" (v. 5). For Jewish captives, this was a radical change. Their religion demanded a strict kosher diet, and the Babylonian menu violated their previous dietary laws.

4. *Change their loyalty.* This was the most radical step. The Babylonians attempted to change the captives' religious loyalty from Jehovah to the gods of the Babylonians. They did this by giving Daniel and his friends new names. Both their Jewish and Babylonian names had significant meanings.

> Among these were some from Judah: Daniel, Hananiah, Mishael and Azariah. The chief official gave them new names: to Daniel, the name Belteshazzar; to Hananiah, Shadrach; to Mishael, Meshach; and to Azariah, Abednego.
>
> Daniel 1:6–7

Daniel's name was changed to Belteshazzar.
        Daniel—God is my judge
        Belteshazzar—may Bel protect his life

Hananiah's name was changed to Shadrach.

    Hananiah—Jehovah is gracious

    Shadrach—command of Aku (moon god)

Mishael's name was changed to Meshach.

    Mishael—who is like God

    Meshach—who is like Aku (moon god)

Azariah's name was changed to Abednego.

    Azariah—the Lord helps

    Abednego—servant of Nebo (son of Baal)

Insight

The first seven verses of this first chapter introduce us to Daniel and the circumstances he faced. Yet from these introductory comments there are a number of important practical insights.

1. *God is the God of human history.* God was not isolated from the events that brought Daniel to Babylon, nor is he isolated from the events of the world in which we live. God is alive and active in history. God did not just create the world and let it go. He created it and sustains it. Nations rise and fall according to his will (see Rom. 13:1). The hearts of political leaders are in his hand (see Prov. 21:1). He uses pagan powers to do his will (see Isa. 10:5).

2. *We are all under pressure to conform to the world.* Daniel and his friends faced incredible pressure. Everything was changing—their language, their reading, their diet, and their names. The objective of the Babylonians was to make them look like, talk like, think like, dress like, eat like, and be like the Babylonians. It was a deliberate attempt to cut them off from their cultural and religious roots. As believers, we face similar pressures today. First, we belong to God's family, and we have our own language, literature, lifestyle, and loyalty. Second, the world continues to pressure us to break our loyalty and adapt to its language, literature, lifestyle, and loyalties. The following chart illustrates the differences:

Language

Christianity

Do not let any unwholesome talk come out of your mouths, but only what is helpful for building others up according to their needs, that it may benefit those who listen. And do not grieve the Holy Spirit of God, with whom you were sealed for the day of redemption. Get rid of all bitterness, rage and anger, brawling and slander, along with every form of malice. Be kind and compassionate to one another, forgiving each other, just as in Christ God forgave you.

Ephesians 4:29–32

The World

Their throats are open graves; their tongues practice deceit.
The poison of vipers is on their lips.
Their mouths are full of cursing and bitterness.
Their feet are swift to shed blood;
ruin and misery mark their ways,
and the way of peace they do not know.
There is no fear of God before their eyes.

Romans 3:13–18

Literature

Christianity

Finally, brothers, whatever is true, whatever is noble, whatever is right, whatever is pure, whatever is lovely, whatever is admirable— if anything is excellent or praiseworthy—think about such things. Whatever you have learned or received or heard from me, or seen in me—put it into practice. And the God of peace will be with you.

Philippians 4:8–9

The World

For although they knew God, they neither glorified him as God nor gave thanks to him, but their thinking became futile and their foolish hearts were darkened. Although they claimed to be wise, they became fools and exchanged the glory of the immortal God for images made to look like mortal man and birds and animals and reptiles. Therefore God gave them over in the sinful desires of their hearts to sexual impurity for the degrading of their bodies with one another.

Romans 1:21–24

Lifestyle

Christianity

Therefore, I urge you, brothers, in view of God's mercy, to offer your bodies as living sacrifices, holy and pleasing to God—this is your spiritual act of worship. Do not conform any longer to the pattern of this world, but be transformed by the renewing of your mind. Then you will be able to test and approve what God's will is—his good, pleasing and perfect will.

Romans 12:1–2

The World

Furthermore, since they did not think it worthwhile to retain the knowledge of God, he gave them over to a depraved mind, to do what ought not to be done. They have become filled with every kind of wickedness, evil, greed and depravity. They are full of envy, murder, strife, deceit and malice. They are gossips, slanderers, God-haters, insolent, arrogant and boastful; they invent ways of doing evil; they disobey their parents; they are senseless, faithless, heartless, ruthless. Although they know God's righteous decree that those who do such things deserve death, they not only continue to do these very things but also approve of those who practice them.

Romans 1:28–32

Loyalty

Christianity

But seek first his kingdom and his righteousness, and all these things will be given to you as well.

Matthew 6:33

The World

You belong to your father, the devil, and you want to carry out your father's desire. He was a murderer from the beginning, not holding to the truth, for there is no truth in him. When he lies, he speaks his native language, for he is a liar and the father of lies.

John 8:44

3. *It's not easy to take a stand.* Daniel and his friends were faced with difficult choices. How should they respond to this pressure? If they decide to take a stand, where should they draw the line?

- Should they refuse to learn the language?
- Should they refuse to read the literature?
- Should they decline the fancy foods?
- Should they refuse their new names?
- Should they keep their mouths shut?

What would you do? Would you take a stand? If so, on what issue and to what degree?

Prayer

Lord, in times of upheaval and change, I am thankful that you are alive and involved. So I thank you for our president, his cabinet, Congress, and state and local leaders. Reveal your purposes through them. I confess that I constantly feel the pressure to conform to the world around me. Deliver me from bad language, and sexist, racial, or dirty jokes. Keep my language pure. All around me the messages of media and literature force anti-Christian values. Help me to reject them. Give me wisdom in making lifestyle choices so that others will see my loyalty to you. I yield my life to you today. Amen.

Chapter Two

Just Say No

Daniel 1:8–21

Sometimes it is easy to say "no"; at other times it is not. *No* is a frequently used word in the vocabulary of parents. "No, no," we tell little children. "Can I stay out late tonight?" our teenager asks. "No," we respond without much thought. "But why not?" "Don't ask why not—the answer is no!" For parents "no" comes easier than "yes." At other times, however, "no" is difficult to say. This is especially true when we are under pressure to say "yes."

One of Satan's strategies is to get us to say "yes" to sin. In fact, this was his temptation in the Garden of Eden. God had given Adam and Eve clear instructions about the garden. He told them they could eat freely of the fruit of all the trees except the tree of the knowledge of good and evil. They were to say "no" to the fruit of that tree. But Satan came along, and Adam and Eve said "yes" instead of "no." Satan has not changed his strategy since the garden. He wants us to say "yes" to temptation. This is the pressure that Daniel faces.

Daniel and several friends from Jerusalem have been taken to Babylon to serve in the court of Nebuchadnezzar. When he arrives he is put on a three-year training program. He is to learn the language of the Babylonians. He is to learn the literature of the Babylonians. He is to adopt a new lifestyle, and his Hebrew name is changed. All of this is designed to restructure his thinking. And Daniel is between fourteen and nineteen when he faces these pressures in a foreign country.

Taking a Stand Involves a Choice

> But Daniel resolved not to defile himself with the royal food and wine, and he asked the chief official for permission not to defile himself this way.
>
> Daniel 1:8

The key word is the verb *resolved*. This Hebrew verb is used several ways in the Old Testament. In Isaiah 42:25 it is translated "take it to heart":

> So he poured out on them his
>   burning anger,
>   the violence of war.
> It enveloped them in flames, yet
>   they did not understand;
>   it consumed them, but they did
>   not take it to heart.

They did not take God's judgment *to heart*. They did not take it seriously. In Malachi 2:2 the verb is used in connection with God's people:

> "If you do not listen, and if you do not set your heart to honor my name," says the LORD Almighty, "I will send a curse upon you, and I will curse your blessings. Yes, I have already cursed them, because you have not set your heart to honor me."

Here the verb is translated "set your heart." It means to set a clear objective and establish an important priority.

The verb is used twice in Isaiah 57.

> The righteous perish,
>   and no one ponders it in his
>   heart;
> devout men are taken away,
>   and no one understands
> that the righteous are taken away
>   to be spared from evil.
>
> verse 1

Whom have you so dreaded and
   feared
  that you have been false to me,
and have neither remembered me
   nor pondered this in your hearts?
Is it not because I have long been
   silent
  that you do not fear me?
                               verse 11

Here it is translated with the idea of pondering something in one's heart. It means to meditate on something, think it over, think it through. When you merge these passages, you get a basic idea of what it means to be "resolved." Daniel thought this issue over and pondered it in his heart. He concluded that this was an important and compelling issue. It was a priority. He took it seriously. And he said "no."

Taking a Stand Involves Drawing a Line

Daniel had to decide on which issues he would take a stand. He had several options.

- Should he refuse to learn the Babylonian language?
- Should he refuse to learn the Babylonian literature?
- Should he refuse the food and wine?
- Should he refuse a Babylonian name?

My personal recommendation to Daniel would have been to *first* refuse the Babylonian literature. After all, this would pollute his mind with pagan ideas and morals. Second, I would recommend refusing a pagan name. Third, I would recommend refusing the Babylonian language. And of *least* importance, refuse the food and wine.

Daniel makes a choice. He refuses the food and wine, and he gives a reason for his choice: "And he asked the chief official for permission not to defile himself this way" (Dan. 1:8). Daniel draws the line on this issue because failure to do so would have been disobedience to God. Eating all of the king's meat would have violated God's commands in regard to acceptable and nonacceptable food. The issue of meat was clear-cut. But the issue of wine was not clear-cut. There was no prohi-

bition against drinking wine. In fact, the consumption of wine was associated with temple worship (see Deut. 14:22–27). Yet Daniel chooses
to abstain. Why? Probably because Babylonian culture was dominated
by the use and abuse of alcohol. So Daniel decides to take a radical
stand in two ways. First, he refuses *all* meat, not just unclean meat. Second, he refuses wine even though it was not prohibited. The lesson we
learn is that being in a pagan culture demands radical choices.

Wheaties and Water

In verse 8 of chapter 1 we read that Daniel "resolved." In verse 9 we
read, "Now God had caused." When we take a radical, right, and courageous stand, we can be sure that God is at work. God granted Daniel
favor (kindness) and sympathy (tender love) with his supervisor. But the
supervisor has a problem. He is responsible for Daniel's well-being, and
if he fails—well, he will not get demoted; he will get beheaded. He is
sympathetic to Daniel, but his neck (literally) is on the line. So Daniel
offers a compromise—a win-win proposal.

> Daniel then said to the guard whom the chief official had appointed over
> Daniel, Hananiah, Mishael and Azariah, "Please test your servants for ten
> days: Give us nothing but vegetables to eat and water to drink. Then com-
> pare our appearance with that of the young men who eat the royal food,
> and treat your servants in accordance with what you see." So he agreed to
> this and tested them for ten days.
>
> Daniel 1:11–14

What a lousy diet. Vegetables and water. No steak. No chicken. No
chocolate. No ice cream. Just broccoli and water (or Wheaties and water).
Wheaties with Nebuchadnezzar's picture on the box. This diet must seem
foolish to everyone else except Daniel and his friends. For them it is obedience to God. They are testing God.

The Wisdom of God

> To these four young men God gave knowledge and understanding of all
> kinds of literature and learning. And Daniel could understand visions and
> dreams of all kinds.
>
> Daniel 1:17

There were three observable and undeniable consequences to this experiment. Two of the results are immediate and one is long-term. First, God gives them knowledge and understanding. He gives them clarity of thought and additional understanding of Babylonian literature and learning. Second, Daniel is given a supernatural ability to understand and interpret dreams and visions. Third, Daniel is given a position of influence in the kingdom.

> [God] changes times and seasons;
>   he sets up kings and deposes
>   them.
> He gives wisdom to the wise
>   and knowledge to the discerning.
>   Daniel 2:21

Daniel's influence extends for seventy years, from the reign of Nebuchadnezzar to the reign of Cyrus.

God blesses and honors Daniel's radical choice. Because Daniel is true to God and says "no," God honors and blesses him. We are told that after being examined by Nebuchadnezzar, Daniel and his friends are "ten times better than all the magicians and enchanters in his whole kingdom" (Dan. 1:20). Daniel offers a ten-day experimental diet, and God makes him ten times better than anyone else in regard to wisdom and understanding. Ten for ten.

Insight

1. *God is not removed from the events of human history.* Many people think of God as an old man with a long white beard. He is sitting in a rocking chair on a distant planet. He sits and observes the events on planet earth. This picture of God implies that he is old, helpless, out-of-date, and completely uninvolved in the events of the twentieth century. Nothing could be further from the truth. God was active in Daniel's day, and he is active in our day. In this first chapter of Daniel, his activity is mentioned three times.

In the first place, God delivers the nation of Judah into the hand of Nebuchadnezzar.

And the Lord delivered Jehoiakim king of Judah into his hand, along with some of the articles from the temple of God. These he carried off to the temple of his god in Babylonia and put in the treasure house of his god.

Daniel 1:2

God is involved in the rising and falling of political powers. He is involved in allowing bad things to happen to his people. Even pagan kings do the bidding of God.

Second, God not only directs the affairs of nations, he also is involved at a personal level in the lives of human beings. "Now God had caused the official to show favor and sympathy to Daniel" (Dan. 1:9). This official is not a believer. He is not a follower of Daniel's God. Yet God works in his life and *causes* him to show favor to Daniel. God is at work in human history through people's lives—even those who do not acknowledge him.

In the third place, God is also at work in the lives of his children.

To these four young men God gave knowledge and understanding of all kinds of literature and learning. And Daniel could understand visions and dreams of all kinds.

Daniel 1:17

God grants wisdom and understanding to Daniel and his friends.

The God we serve is not outdated or out of touch. He is very much involved in both history and the people who make up history. Daniel understands this well. In the second chapter he offers a prayer to God. The first part of the prayer deals with God's activity in the events of human history.

Praise be to the name of God for
    ever and ever;
    wisdom and power are his.
He changes times and seasons;
    he sets up kings and deposes
      them.
He gives wisdom to the wise
    and knowledge to the discerning.
He reveals deep and hidden things;
    he knows what lies in darkness,
    and light dwells with him.

Daniel 2:20–22

The second part of the prayer acknowledges that God is also involved at a personal level in the lives of people.

> I thank and praise you, O God of
>   my fathers:
>   You have given me wisdom and
>   power,
>   you have made known to me what
>   we asked of you,
>   you have made known to us the
>   dream of the king.
>   Daniel 2:23

What does that mean for us today? It does not absolve us of human responsibility. It does not mean, "Well, since God is in control and since God is involved in the events of human history, I can just sit back and do nothing. After all, Jesus is coming. So I don't have to worry about anything." Not at all! Daniel is not fatalistic. He works. He prays. He influences. He takes his stand. And God works in the circumstances he faces and brings about some miracles. It does mean that whatever happens, I have an inner confidence that God is in control. He is in control of the nations, nonbelieving individuals, and my own life. God is never surprised. God never says, "Oops!"

2. *God desires obedience.* The second insight from the first chapter is that whatever the circumstances, God desires obedience on our part. That obedience is our responsibility. We must make the choice. Daniel has to make a choice.

> But Daniel resolved not to defile himself with the royal food and wine, and he asked the chief official for permission not to defile himself this way.
>   Daniel 1:8

God does not make the choice for him. His friends do not make the choice for him. He has to make the choice.

The same is true in our lives. God has outlined his desires for us in the Bible. He has already given us his expectations. Now the choice is up to us. It's really a simple choice—it is "yes" or "no." It is "I will obey" or "I will not obey." There is no middle ground.

3. *We must obey God whatever the consequences.* This story has a happy ending. Daniel takes a courageous stand. They put him to the

test for ten days. He passes the test with an A+. They decide that instead of feeding him the king's food and wine, they will give him vegetables and water. At the end of the three-year period, he is ten times better than all of the other people in the king's training program. God gives him insight, and he is placed in a position of influence in the kingdom. Daniel influences that kingdom and the succeeding empires for seventy years. He obeys God. He takes a courageous stand. And everything turns out wonderfully!

But it does not always work out that way. Sometimes you take a stand for God, and as a result you lose your job. Sometimes you take a stand for God, and you lose all your friends. Sometimes you take a stand for God, and suffer financial or personal loss. Doing right does not guarantee a good result. But we are to do right whatever the consequences.

The eleventh chapter of Hebrews describes people who took a stand for God. Sometimes it turned out good. Sometimes it did not.

And what more shall I say? I do not have time to tell about Gideon, Barak, Samson, Jephthah, David, Samuel and the prophets, who through faith conquered kingdoms, administered justice, and gained what was promised; who shut the mouths of lions, quenched the fury of the flames, and escaped the edge of the sword; whose weakness was turned to strength; and who became powerful in battle and routed foreign armies.

Hebrews 11:32–34

For others the outcome was different. They took a stand for God and were persecuted and killed.

Others were tortured and refused to be released, so that they might gain a better resurrection. Some faced jeers and flogging, while still others were chained and put in prison. They were stoned; they were sawed in two; they were put to death by the sword. They went about in sheepskins and goatskins, destitute, persecuted and mistreated—the world was not worthy of them. They wandered in deserts and mountains, and in caves and holes in the ground.

Hebrews 11:35–38

From the first chapter of Daniel we learn that God is involved in the circumstances of human history, therefore, we can trust him. It is our choice to make—to obey God whatever the consequences of the obedience.

Prayer

Dear God, all of life is making choices. Help me to make the choices that would please you. Give me the same courage that Daniel had. Help me to stand alone, if necessary. Help me to stand against all the pressures that would force me to disobey you. I trust you to work in my life as I follow and obey you. Help me to obey you even when I know it will not turn out for my benefit. Amen.

Chapter Three

What to Do When There Is Nothing You Can Do

Daniel 2:1–19

When I was in college I developed some medical problems that put me in the hospital for five weeks. The doctors ran many tests and gave me all kinds of medicine, but the problem continued. Then a specialist was brought in who told me I had a tumor—and it was most likely cancerous. He would not know for sure until he operated. He gave me temporary permission to leave the hospital for a day, and then I was to return to have the surgery.

I went to the college cafeteria to eat that night. Everyone was laughing, talking, and planning for the weekend ahead. It was as if life was passing me by and nobody cared. I wanted to stop all the talking and tell everybody about my medical problems, but instead I silently watched my friends. I felt lonely. I also felt helpless. There was *nothing* I could do but wait. As it turned out I had neither a tumor nor cancer, but I will never forget the complete feeling of helplessness. There was nothing I could do.

This is the kind of situation that Daniel now faces. He is confronted with an impossible task, and he doesn't know what to do.

The Troubling Dream

> In the second year of his reign, Nebuchadnezzar had dreams; his mind
> was troubled and he could not sleep.
>
> Daniel 2:1

Before we examine the king's problem, we need to deal with an apparent contradiction in the text. The second chapter begins with the Hebrew conjunction *and*. This implies that the events of chapter 2 follow in historical sequence to the events of chapter 1. Herein lies the problem. In chapter 1 the Hebrew slaves are to be trained for three years (see Dan. 1:5). At the end of the three years they are examined by the king and then admitted into political service (see Dan. 1:18). At the end of chapter 1 Nebuchadnezzar has been king for at least three years. However, chapter 2 begins, "In the second year of his reign." The answer to this dilemma is found in a proper understanding of how the Babylonians counted the reign of a king. They counted as follows:

The first year was called the Year of Ascension.
The second year was called the first year after ascension.
The third year was called the second year after ascension, etc.

Consequently when chapter 2 begins, "in the second year," it is likely referring to the second year after the Year of Ascension. Therefore, by our counting system, it would be his third year, which is precisely what is stated in chapter 1.

During this year, Nebuchadnezzar has dreams. His mind is troubled. This implies a deep disturbance that brings anxiety and apprehension. Because of this, he cannot sleep. The Hebrew text literally states that sleep went away from him. We have all experienced sleepless nights. We keep chasing after sleep and the harder we try the further away it gets from us.

When You Are Not Sure What to Do—
Call a Consultant

Nebuchadnezzar does what kings do when they have a problem. He calls in the consultants—the people who are experts in dealing with this kind of situation.

So the king summoned the magicians, enchanters, sorcerers and astrologers to tell him what he had dreamed. When they came in and stood before the king, he said to them, "I have had a dream that troubles me and I want to know what it means."

Daniel 2:2–3

The magicians are learned in the sacred writings of the Babylonians. They will provide spiritual insight. The enchanters are probably experts in communicating with the dead. Their title comes from a verb that means to breathe or whisper. If the dreams carry a message from the dead, then the enchanters will be able to decipher it. The sorcerers are workers of magic. They specialize in spells, potions, and formulas. If this is required to understand the dreams, then the sorcerers can deliver. The astrologers (literally Chaldeans) are experts in reading the stars. Their understanding of great cosmic events might give the proper perspective on the king's dreams. If anyone can help the king, this group of consultants can. The king narrows his interest to one dream (see v. 3) and asks them to explain what it means.

MBI (Management by Intimidation)

The consultants make a reasonable request of the king. "O king, live forever! Tell your servants the dream, and we will interpret it" (v. 4). No consultant can work without an adequate database. Nobody can interpret a dream until they know what the dream was. However, this is not what Nebuchadnezzar has in mind.

The king replied to the astrologers, "This is what I have firmly decided: If you do not tell me what my dream was and interpret it, I will have you cut into pieces and your houses turned into piles of rubble. But if you tell me the dream and explain it, you will receive from me gifts and rewards and great honor. So tell me the dream and interpret it for me."

Daniel 2:5–6

There are a variety of ways to manage people. One popular way is MBWA (Management by Walking About). This was popularized in the best-selling book *In Search of Excellence* by Peters and Waterman. It is a style of management that encourages a supervisor to get out of the office and walk around among the employees. Another popular management style is MBO (Management by Objective). You set your objectives and then you structure yourself and your organization to meet those objectives. You manage by continually keeping the objectives in mind.

Nebuchadnezzar introduces another style. It is MBI (Management by Intimidation). He decides that the consultants must tell him the dream and interpret it. If they don't, they will be "cut into pieces" (v. 5). This is not metaphorical language—it is a real threat. On the other hand, if they can tell him the dream and interpret it, they will receive "gifts and rewards and great honor" (v. 6). If I had been one of these consultants, I would have immediately updated my resume and requested a transfer to another department. But this was not an option for them.

Nebuchadnezzar Ain't Stupid

Why did Nebuchadnezzar insist on the impossible? Some commentators think that Nebuchadnezzar had forgotten the dream. In fact the King James Version translates verse 5 this way: "The king answered and said to the Chaldeans, The thing is gone from me." The New International Version translates the same verse, "The king replied to the astrologers, 'This is what I have firmly decided.'" The verb that is translated here is *azda*, which means "to go forth." It has two possible ideas. First, "to go forth" in the sense of leaving and being forgotten. Second, "to go forth" in the sense of setting something forth or making a declaration. I favor the second idea (as do the translators of the NIV).

Apparently the king is testing his advisers. He has "firmly decided" that they will tell him the dream and interpret it. Perhaps these advisers were his father's advisers, and he is testing their knowledge and loyalty. In fact, Nebuchadnezzar implies this in his anger when they cannot tell him the dream.

> Then the king answered, "I am certain that you are trying to gain time, because you realize that this is what I have firmly decided: If you do not tell me the dream, there is just one penalty for you. You have conspired to tell me misleading and wicked things, hoping the situation will change. So then, tell me the dream, and I will know that you can interpret it for me."
>
> Daniel 2:8–9

To Dream the Impossible Dream

This is a story of increasing intensity. It starts with a simple request. Nebuchadnezzar wants his dream interpreted. "No problem," say the wise men. The king then wants the wise men to tell him the dream and then interpret it. "Big problem," say the wise men. Then the king raises the intensity to the highest level. "If you don't tell me the dream and interpret it, you die," he says. Finally the wise men get honest.

> The astrologers answered the king, "There is not a man on earth who can do what the king asks! No king, however great and mighty, has ever asked such a thing of any magician or enchanter or astrologer. What the king asks is too difficult. No one can reveal it to the king except the gods, and they do not live among men."
>
> Daniel 2:10–11

This seems like a reasonable (and honest) answer, but it has two major problems. First, their answer plays right into the ego of Nebuchadnezzar. The king already believes that he is the greatest and mightiest king who ever lived. The answer of the astrologers confirms this in his mind. They say, "No king, however great and mighty, has ever asked such a thing of any magician or enchanter or astrologer" (v. 10). Do you know what the king is likely thinking? "If this is true that no one has ever asked this before, then I can't back off because it confirms that I am the greatest and mightiest." In language similar to that of Muhammad Ali, who predicted taking his opponent in eight rounds, the king says,

Neb the great
Takes the astrologers in eight.

The second problem in the answer of the wise men is that they confess the emptiness of their own religion. They say, "No one can reveal it to the king except the gods, and they do not live among men" (v. 11). Nebuchadnezzar is probably thinking, "If the gods don't live among us, what good are they? Maybe we ought to get rid of them and the wise men who promote them."

Help

So far Daniel has been oblivious to the events confronting the wise men. He was not called in to the king nor is he aware that the king has ordered the execution of *all* the wise men (see 2:12).

> So the decree was issued to put the wise men to death, and men were sent to look for Daniel and his friends to put them to death. When Arioch, the commander of the king's guard, had gone out to put to death the wise men of Babylon, Daniel spoke to him with wisdom and tact.
>
> Daniel 2:13–14

What fascinates me in this story is that when they come to kill Daniel, he responds with great calm and restraint. The text says that Daniel answers the commander of the king's guard (who was there to execute Daniel) with "wisdom and tact" (v. 14). He then goes before the king and asks for time (see 2:16). Daniel is granted additional time even though the king was unwilling to grant additional time to the other wise men. In fact, he accused the others of stalling for time. "I am certain that you are trying to gain time," he said to them (2:8). Yet he is willing to give time to Daniel. Why? He probably sensed a sincere and honest attitude in Daniel.

Everybody Needs a Few Good Friends to Pray for Them

It is one thing to get a stay of execution, but it is another thing to be able to tell and interpret the king's dream. The good news is that Daniel has avoided death. The bad news is that if he doesn't come up with the dream and an interpretation, he is going to die anyway. At this point it appears that there is nothing Daniel can do but wait impending execution along with all the wise men of Babylon. But there is something he can do, and what he can do, he does. He gets his friends together and commits the matter to God in prayer.

> Then Daniel returned to his house and explained the matter to his friends Hananiah, Mishael and Azariah. He urged them to plead for mercy from the God of heaven concerning this mystery, so that he and his friends might not be executed with the rest of the wise men of Babylon.
>
> Daniel 2:17–18

Daniel is facing an impossible situation, and he responds to it by sharing it with God and with a few faithful friends. The same ought to be true in our own lives. When there is nothing you can do, you can do something. You can pray to God and share your burden with a few faithful friends who can pray as well.

First, give your burden to God. "Cast all your anxiety on him because he cares for you" (1 Peter 5:7).

Second, share it with others. "Carry each other's burdens, and in this way you will fulfill the law of Christ" (Gal. 6:2).

Daniel faces the impossible. He shares it with his friends and "urged them to plead for mercy from the God of heaven" (Dan. 2:18). And then, he goes to bed. Imagine that. He is facing death, and he goes to sleep. While this may appear strange to us—sleeping when you are about to die—it is not strange for Daniel. After all, he has prayed and shared his burden with God. He has left it in God's hands. There is nothing more he can do, so why worry? He goes to bed and "during the night the mystery was revealed to Daniel in a vision. Then Daniel praised the God of heaven" (Dan. 2:19).

Insight

1. *It all depends on your point of view.* From a human standpoint, this is a story of hopelessness. Nebuchadnezzar has asked the impossible. The astrologers are absolutely correct in their assessment of the situation. "There is not a man on earth who can do what the king asks" (2:10). Yet Daniel has a different point of view. His perspective includes the God of heaven who can intervene in the circumstances of human history and perform a miracle. The astrologers are circumstance-centered. Daniel is God-centered. He demonstrates his God-centered view in three ways:

1. He prays to God (2:18).
2. He praises God (2:20–23).
3. Later, he gives God the credit (2:27–28).

2. *Everyone needs a few good friends to pray for them.* Daniel does not face this crisis alone. He faces it with Hananiah, Mishael, and Azariah—his friends. In a crisis we all need a few good friends who will stand with us and pray for us. My wife and my children are part of my friendship circle that keeps me in line and prays for me. The board of our

church is another circle that holds me accountable for my ministry, corrects me when I need correction, encourages me when I need encouragement, but most of all that prays for me in all of the struggles that I face every day. Then I have a very small group of personal, intimate, long-term friends whom I can go to when I have nowhere else to turn, and I find in them strength, wisdom, and encouragement. We pray for each other every day. Believers need a few good friends to keep them on track.

Prayer

Dear God, as I face the impossible situations of life and there is nothing I can do, remind me that there is something I can do. I can pray. Help me to see above my circumstances so that I can gain your perspective. I thank you for the friends you have brought into my life. I pray for them in their own spiritual journeys and struggles. Thank you for not leaving me alone down here. You are with me and so are my friends. Amen.

Chapter Four

How Big Is Your God?

Daniel 2:20–23

Daniel is faced with an impossible situation. King Nebuchadnezzar has had a dream, and he wants his wise men to interpret it for him. In order to insure their honesty, Nebuchadnezzar refuses to tell them the content of the dream. He asks them to come up with the content and the interpretation of the dream. Because the wise men are unable to do this, the king orders their execution along with all the wise men in Babylon, including Daniel and his Hebrew friends.

When they come to kill Daniel, Daniel requests some time to respond to the king's dream. The time is granted, and Daniel and his friends pray to God. During the night, God reveals the dream and its interpretation to Daniel in a vision. Daniel immediately responds to God in a hymn of praise (see Dan. 2:20–23).

The Forming of Character

Daniel is a remarkable young man. His life is characterized by a total faith in God even when faced with impossible circumstances. This kind of faith is forged over time. Where did Daniel learn such faith, and how did he develop such character? It appears that this was cultivated and developed through the influence of his parents, historical events, and theology.

The Influence of His Parents

The Scripture tells us little about Daniel's parents or their influence on his life. The one clear contribution that they made was giving Daniel a biblically based name. The name *Daniel* means "God is my judge." It was customary for believing parents to name their children after God. So we know that his parents were committed to God, and they gave him a name connected with God. Wherever he went in life, that name would go with him.

The Influence of Historical Events

We are all influenced by the events we experience. I can remember where I was when two major events happened. If you are around forty years of age, you are probably in the same category. I remember exactly where I was and precisely what I was doing when I heard that President Kennedy had been assassinated. Do you remember that? That is etched forever in my memory. I was in Ireland at the time. My Aunt Mary was baby-sitting. We were listening to the BBC in the evening when the news of his assassination was announced. The second event I remember is the first time I heard the Beatles. Now that's a very spiritual event! But if you are around my age, you probably remember exactly where you were the first time you heard them sing. We are all shaped by events that impact our lives.

The same was true for Daniel. Remember that Daniel was part of the royal family in Palestine. As part of that family, he observed some incredible events that undoubtedly shaped his life, values, and character. For most of Daniel's life in Palestine, King Josiah was on the throne. "Josiah was seven years old when he became king, and he reigned in Jerusalem forty years" (2 Chron. 24:1).

Daniel was born after Josiah had been king for about sixteen years.

In the eighth year of his reign, while he was still young, he began to seek the God of his father David. In his twelfth year he began to purge Judah and Jerusalem of high places, Asherah poles, carved idols and cast images. Under his direction the altars of the Baals were torn down; he cut to pieces the incense altars that were above them, and smashed the Asherah poles, the idols and the images. These he broke to pieces and scattered over the graves of those who had sacrificed to them.

2 Chronicles 34:3–4

The land was purified in Josiah's eighteenth year as king. Daniel was three or four years old at this time.

> While they were bringing out the money that had been taken into the temple of the LORD, Hilkiah the priest found the Book of the Law of the LORD that had been given through Moses. . . .
>
> When the king heard the words of the Law, he tore his robes. He gave these orders to Hilkiah, Ahikam son of Shaphan, Abdon son of Micah, Shaphan the secretary and Asaiah the king's attendant: "Go and inquire of the LORD for me and for the remnant in Israel and Judah about what is written in this book that has been found. Great is the LORD's anger that is poured out on us because our fathers have not kept the word of the LORD; they have not acted in accordance with all that is written in this book."
>
> 2 Chronicles 34:14, 19–21

Daniel lived through an incredible period of revival. Just as I remember significant historical events, Daniel likewise remembered the remarkable work of God.

The Influence of Theology

Theology has fallen on hard times these days. We are more interested in experience, pragmatism, and self-satisfaction than we are in theology. For many in evangelical circles, the focus has become counselors rather than God. This is reflected in the content of our preaching, the words of our music, and the focus of the programs we promote. Daniel's character was shaped by his theology. He had a biblical, sound, high view of God. It was his high view of God that sustained him in the crises of life—including the possibility of execution.

Let God Be God

One of the reasons we live defeated lives is that we try to deal with the problems of life on our own. We fail to let God be God. When God answers Daniel's prayer and reveals Nebuchadnezzar's dream to him, he responds with a prayer of praise to God. The content of the prayer indicates that Daniel not only understands who God is and what God can do, but he is willing to trust this God completely.

The prayer begins, "Praise be to the name of God for ever and ever" (Dan. 2:20). This is the first time in the Old Testament that the words "for ever and ever" are used, and they are used in reference to God. Daniel understands that God is not limited by time and space. When we face our mountaintop of problems, we think that the entire universe centers around the crisis we face. Daniel faces a real crisis, but he looks beyond the problem (he is facing death) and recognizes that the God he knows is bigger than his mountain. God's perspective is eternal.

Daniel then identifies two main characteristics of God—wisdom and power (see 2:20). *Wisdom* is God's insight, perspective, and will for human beings and human history. *Power* is his ability to execute his wisdom and will for human beings and human history. These two characteristics become the basis for the rest of the prayer (Dan. 2:21).

1. The power of God: "He changes times and seasons; he sets up kings and deposes them."
2. The wisdom of God: "He gives wisdom to the wise and knowledge to the discerning."

Daniel then concludes his prayer on a personal note. He has described God as a God of power and wisdom. He has talked about that power and wisdom in the universe. Now he brings it down into his own life.

> I thank and praise you, O God of
>   my fathers:
> You have given me wisdom and
>   power,
> you have made known to me what
>   we asked of you,
> you have made known to us the
>   dream of the king.
>   Daniel 2:23

Insight

1. *It is not the size of your problem that counts, it is your view of God.* Daniel faced the ultimate mountain. He needed a miracle from God, or he and his friends would be executed. Daniel had a godly perspective.

He knew that as big as the problem was, God was bigger. David writes about this in the Book of Psalms.

> I love you, O LORD, my strength.
> The LORD is my rock, my fortress
>   and my deliverer;
>   my God is my rock, in whom I
>   take refuge.
> He is my shield and the horn of
>   my salvation, my stronghold.
> I call to the LORD, who is worthy of
>   praise,
>   and I am saved from my enemies.
>   Psalm 18:1–3

A number of years ago we vacationed at a dude ranch in Colorado. The ranch where we lived for that week was in a little valley surrounded by the Rocky Mountains. Everywhere we turned we were surrounded by the mountains. It appeared to me that the mountains we saw from the meadow were the only mountains in the world. I felt so overwhelmed by the beauty and dignity of these mountains. Then we would get on a horse and ride to the top of one of those mountains. And you know what? There were more mountains beyond those mountains. I remember sitting on a rock as the guides pointed out Pike's Peak in the distance and said, "At the foot of Pike's Peak is Colorado Springs, and over there beyond those mountains is Denver." And then beyond that is Kansas, and Missouri, and the United States, and the world, and the universe. But down in the valley it all seems so limited and so confined and so surrounded.

How do you think God sees things? Certainly not down in the valley bound and shaped by time and space. God is far bigger. God is the God of eternity. Wisdom is learning to see things from God's point of view! God is our rock. He is our fortress. He is our deliverer. He is our strength. He is our power. He is our wisdom. God is far bigger than any problem you face today! It's not the size of the mountain—it's your view of God.

Read Psalm 18:1–3 again. Except this time put *your* name in the psalm.

> I love you, O LORD, Ed's strength.
> The LORD is Ed's rock, Ed's fortress
>   and Ed's deliverer;

> Ed's God is Ed's rock, in whom Ed
>   takes refuge.
> He is Ed's shield and the horn of
>   Ed's salvation, Ed's stronghold.
> Ed calls to the LORD, who is worthy of
>   praise,
> and Ed is saved from Ed's enemies.

2. *In the crises of life, we need wisdom and power*. In the midst of life's difficulties, we need two things—wisdom and power.

Wisdom is seeing things from God's point of view. If that is critical, then how do we get such wisdom? We get it from reading, studying, and memorizing the Scriptures. Where did Daniel receive his wisdom? From the Scriptures. Almost the entire content of his prayer comes from the Book of Psalms. Daniel was versed in the Word of God. More than that, he had committed the Psalms to memory. He knew the prayers and the praises of Old Testament Israel. When he faced an unbelievable crisis, he received wisdom from God because he had already committed to memory passages of Scripture from the Word of God.

How do we get God's power? Through prayer.

> If any of you lacks wisdom, he should ask God, who gives generously to all without finding fault, and it will be given to him. But when he asks, he must believe and not doubt, because he who doubts is like a wave of the sea, blown and tossed by the wind.
>
> James 1:5–6

> In my distress I called to the LORD;
>   I cried to my God for help.
> From his temple he heard my voice;
>   my cry came before him, into his
>   ears.
>
> Psalm 18:6

> It is God who arms me with
>   strength
> and makes my way perfect.
>
> Psalm 18:32

You give me your shield of victory,
   and your right hand sustains me;
   you stoop down to make me
     great.

                 Psalm 18:35

Recently I was reading the works of Andrew Murray, who suggested that as Christians we need to know four things in every circumstance of life. I've developed a little system for remembering them, paraphrasing Andrew Murray's writings. It is AKT[2].

A—*I am here by God's Appointment.* We have a tendency to lose perspective on that. When everything is going well in our lives, we acknowledge, "Yes, God, you are in control." But when things have fallen apart in our lives and we are facing the crisis, our attitude is: "God if you were in control, this would never have happened." If I understand the Scriptures and understand Daniel's view of God, I must conclude that wherever I am, God is still in control. *A* stands for: I am here by God's appointment. That's wisdom.

K—*I am in his Keeping.* That's his power and strength. Wherever you are as a believer, God is still in control of your life. In his wisdom and his providence he has brought you to these circumstances. You are there by appointment, and you are under his keeping. He has not forsaken you. He has not turned his back on you. You may sit in darkness, but Daniel says God sees what's in the darkness around you. His grace is sufficient. You are there under his keeping.

T—*I am under his Training.* Training is not fun. I remember when I coached soccer at a university. The first couple of weeks were absolute misery for every athlete. If you're an athlete, you understand what I'm talking about. The coach has little compassion—it is *run, run, run.* Training is painful! I am here by God's appointment. I am in his keeping. I am in training. God is doing something unique in my life through these circumstances to make me more like Jesus Christ. I am constantly under his training.

T—*I am here for his Time period.* When will my circumstances change? When God decides it. His time, not my time.

AKT[2]
I am here by Appointment.
I am in his Keeping.
I am under his Training.
I am here for his Time period.

You may want to jot that down on a card and carry it with you this week.

Prayer

The LORD reigns,
  let the nations tremble;
he sits enthroned between the
    cherubim,
  let the earth shake.
Great is the LORD in Zion;
  he is exalted over all the
    nations.
Let them praise your great and
    awesome name—
  he is holy.
The King is mighty, he loves
    justice—
  you have established equity;
in Jacob you have done
  what is just and right.
Exalt the LORD our God
  and worship at his footstool;
  he is holy.
                    Psalm 99:1–5

Father, we acknowledge that we often have a very small view of who you are. We acknowledge at times we are trapped in the valley surrounded by the mountains of despair. Lift us and let us see from your point of view that you are at work in our lives, that you keep us each day, that you are training us, and that you change the times and seasons according to your plan. Help us to trust you, for you have certainly demonstrated to Daniel that you were and are entirely trustworthy. In the name of Jesus Christ we pray. Amen.

Chapter Five

God Is the God of Human History

Daniel 2:24–49

Nebuchadnezzar has had a troubling and disturbing dream. He calls in his wise men and puts them to the test. "Okay, you're wise—then you must do two things," he says. "Number one, you must tell me what my dream is. I'm not going to tell you—you must tell me. Then, number two, after you have told me my dream, you must give the interpretation." Well this is beyond the abilities of the wise men. They respond, "King Nebuchadnezzar, no king however great or mighty has ever made such a request. This is impossible!" Nebuchadnezzar responds, "Impossible or not, you must do it, or I will cut you into pieces." They cannot do it, so their execution is set. The king's guards arrive to kill Daniel, who says, "Why was the decree issued?" The story is explained to Daniel. Daniel gathers his friends together for a prayer meeting, and God answers his prayer. God reveals the dream and the interpretation. Daniel then goes to the king to both tell and interpret the dream.

But There Is a God in Heaven

Daniel replied, "No wise man, enchanter, magician or diviner can explain to the king the mystery he has asked about, but there is a God in heaven who reveals mysteries. He has shown King Nebuchadnezzar what will happen in days to come. Your dream and the visions that passed through your mind as you lay on your bed are these: . . .

Daniel 2:27–28

The wise men had admitted to the king that they could not tell him the dream. They even admitted that this was even beyond the ability of their gods. "What the king asks is too difficult. No one can reveal it to the king except the gods, and they do not live among men" (Dan. 2:11). What the wise men and their gods could not do, Daniel and his God did. And Daniel places the credit where it belongs: "But there is a God in heaven."

This is a powerful reminder when we are faced with difficult or even impossible situations. "But there is a God." When everything goes wrong in your life remember—"But there is a God." I was so intrigued with this idea that I went to the concordance (via computer) and looked up every verse that contained the words *but God*. Here is a selection for your thought and meditation. The words *but God* offer hope. (Italics added to all references.)

Then Israel said to Joseph, "I am about to die, *but God* will be with you and take you back to the land of your fathers."

Genesis 48:21

You intended to harm me, *but God* intended it for good to accomplish what is now being done, the saving of many lives.

Genesis 50:20

So God [KJV says *but God*] led the people around by the desert road toward the Red Sea. The Israelites went up out of Egypt armed for battle.

Exodus 13:18

David stayed in the desert strongholds and in the hills of the Desert of Ziph. Day after day Saul searched for him, *but God* did not give David into his hands.

1 Samuel 23:14

But God will redeem my life from
    the grave;
  he will surely take me to himself.

Psalm 49:15

Surely God [KJV says *But God*] will crush the heads of
    his enemies,
  the hairy crowns of those who go
    on in their sins.

Psalm 68:21

My flesh and my heart may fail,
  but God is the strength of my
    heart
  and my portion forever.

Psalm 73:26

Although the peoples roar like the
    roar of surging waters,
  when he [KJV says *but God*] rebukes them they flee
    far away,
driven before the wind like chaff on
    the hills,
  like tumbleweed before a gale.

Isaiah 17:13

Why does this fellow talk like that? He's blaspheming! Who can forgive
sins *but God* alone?

Mark 2:7

Because the patriarchs were jealous of Joseph, they sold him as a slave
into Egypt. *But God* was with him.

Acts 7:9

He said to them: "You are well aware that it is against our law for a Jew
to associate with a Gentile or visit him. *But God* has shown me that I should
not call any man impure or unclean."

Acts 10:28

But God raised him from the dead.

Acts 13:30

But God demonstrates his own love for us in this: While we were still sinners, Christ died for us.

Romans 5:8

But thanks be to *God* that, [KJV says *But God* be thanked] though you used to be slaves to sin, you wholeheartedly obeyed the form of teaching to which you were entrusted.

Romans 6:17

But God chose the foolish things of the world to shame the wise; God chose the weak things of the world to shame the strong.

1 Corinthians 1:27

But God has revealed it to us by his Spirit. The Spirit searches all things, even the deep things of God.

1 Corinthians 2:10

I planted the seed, Apollos watered it, *but God* made it grow.

1 Corinthians 3:6

No temptation has seized you except what is common to man. *And God* [KJV says *But God*] is faithful; he will not let you be tempted beyond what you can bear. But when you are tempted, he will also provide a way out so that you can stand up under it.

1 Corinthians 10:13

But because of his great love for us, *God* [KJV says *But God*, who is] who is rich in mercy made us alive with Christ.

Ephesians 2:4–5

Indeed he was ill, and almost died. *But God* had mercy on him, and not on him only but also on me, to spare me sorrow upon sorrow.

Philippians 2:27

The Dream

You looked, O king, and there before you stood a large statue—an enormous, dazzling statue, awesome in appearance. The head of the statue was made of pure gold, its chest and arms of silver, its belly and thighs of bronze, its legs of iron, its feet partly of iron and partly of baked clay. While you were watching, a rock was cut out, but not by human hands. It struck the statue on its feet of iron and clay and smashed them. Then the iron, the clay, the bronze, the silver and the gold were broken to pieces at the same time and became like chaff on a threshing floor in the summer.

The wind swept them away without leaving a trace. But the rock that struck
the statue became a huge mountain and filled the whole earth.

Daniel 2:31–35

Before examining the meaning of this dream, there are three important preliminary observations to keep in mind. First, when you move from
the head of the statue to the feet, the quality of the material deteriorates.
Gold—Silver—Bronze—Iron—Clay. Second, as the quality deteriorates,
the strength increases. Third, the various parts of the statue represent
world powers and their influence in human history.

The Head of Gold

This was the dream, and now we will interpret it to the king. You, O king,
are the king of kings. The God of heaven has given you dominion and
power and might and glory; in your hands he has placed mankind and the
beasts of the field and the birds of the air. Wherever they live, he has made
you ruler over them all. You are that head of gold.

Daniel 2:36–38

The head of gold represents Nebuchadnezzar and the Babylonian
Empire. The Babylonians were known for their preference for gold. Nebuchadnezzar wanted to build Babylon as a city of gold. He ruled on a
throne of gold. He built a statue of gold ninety feet high and nine feet
wide. Herodius, who visited Babylon seventy years after Nebuchadnezzar's death noted that he had never seen such an abundance of gold as he
saw in Babylon.

Daniel declared that Nebuchadnezzar has been given "dominion and
power and might and glory; in your hands he has placed mankind and the
beasts of the field and the birds of the air." This would be familiar language to Nebuchadnezzar. Every year in Babylon they celebrated the coming of the new year with a massive festival. Nebuchadnezzar (and the
kings who followed him) would be ushered in and seated upon a throne
of gold. Then there would be a reading of the ancient epic of creation written down by the Babylonians. The people would honor Marduk, their creator god. Then they would worship Nebuchadnezzar as the earthly representative of Marduk. They declared that Nebuchadnezzar ruled not only
peoples, but beasts and animals and birds and all of creation.

The Chest and Arms of Silver

> After you, another kingdom will rise, inferior to yours.
> Daniel 2:39

Very little is said in the text about this next empire, but nearly all Bible scholars agree that it refers to the Medo-Persian Empire. This empire followed the Babylonian Empire. The word for silver in Aramaic is also the word for taxation. When the Medo-Persians came to power, they were known for their extensive system of taxation. All taxes were paid in silver (unlike the Babylonian Empire where taxes were paid in gold). So the silver represents the second world power that would rise to domination.

The Stomach and Thighs of Brass

> Next, a third kingdom, one of bronze [brass], will rule over the whole earth.
> Daniel 2:39

The third kingdom to rule over the whole earth is the Greek Empire. Now if you were living through some of these events, you would better understand the significance of these particular prophecies. If you saw a Medo-Persian soldier, he would be dressed in a cloth turban, a cloth upper tunic with long full arms, and cloth trousers that were full. But when the Greeks came along, their military dress was significantly different. If you saw a Greek soldier, he would have a helmet of brass, a breastplate of brass, a shield of brass, and a sword of brass.

Legs and Feet of Iron

> Finally, there will be a fourth kingdom, strong as iron—for iron breaks and smashes everything—and as iron breaks things to pieces, so it will crush and break all the others. Just as you saw that the feet and toes were partly of baked clay and partly of iron, so this will be a divided kingdom; yet it will have some of the strength of iron in it, even as you saw iron mixed with clay. As the toes were partly iron and partly clay, so this kingdom will be partly strong and partly brittle. And just as you saw the iron mixed with baked clay, so the people will be a mixture and will not remain united, any more than iron mixes with clay.
> Daniel 2:40–43

This fourth kingdom represents the Roman Empire. The iron describes the disciplined beginnings of Roman soldiers who would conquer the known world. More space is devoted to this empire than all the previous ones put together. There are at least two unique characteristics of this empire.

1. *It appears to have two dimensions*. First, the legs are made of pure iron. Second, the toes and feet are made of baked clay and iron. These separate metals are involved in the same empire.

2. *The feet are unique*. The feet are made of a mixture of clay and iron. These elements do not mix into one substance. This would imply a union that maintains separate identities.

> And just as you saw the iron mixed with baked clay, so the people will be a mixture and will not remain united, any more than iron mixes with clay.
>
> Daniel 2:43

This may imply some sort of political or economic cooperation. At the same time, national and cultural identity would be maintained. It will be one empire, but it will be divided.

The Stone Crushes the Feet

> In the time of those kings, the God of heaven will set up a kingdom that will never be destroyed, nor will it be left to another people. It will crush all those kingdoms and bring them to an end, but it will itself endure forever. This is the meaning of the vision of the rock cut out of a mountain, but not by human hands—a rock that broke the iron, the bronze, the clay, the silver and the gold to pieces.
>
> Daniel 2:44–45

There will arise in the events of human history four major world powers: Babylon, Medo-Persia, Greece, and Rome. At some point God will intervene in the events of human history and will crush all previous world powers. God will set up a kingdom. After his kingdom, there will be no other human kingdoms.

Christ Is the Rock

What is the significance of the stone? What or who is this stone? A stone cut without hands. A stone that breaks the feet and crushes the image. A stone that becomes a mountain that encompasses the earth. You have to be very careful that you don't speculate when you come to the Bible. You must allow the Scriptures to interpret themselves whenever possible.

There are two other Old Testament sections that deal with the idea of a stone.

The Rejected Stone

> The stone the builders rejected
>   has become the capstone;
> the LORD has done this,
>   and it is marvelous in our eyes.
>   Psalm 118:22–23

Who is this stone? The New Testament gives us the answer. This passage is quoted twice in the New Testament, and each time, the stone is identified as Jesus Christ. First, Jesus applies this prophecy to himself.

> Jesus looked directly at them and asked, "Then what is the meaning of that which is written:
>
> "'The stone the builders rejected
>   has become the capstone'?"
>   Luke 20:17

Second, Peter applies this verse to Jesus when he addresses the Sanhedrin.

> Then know this, you and all the people of Israel: It is by the name of Jesus Christ of Nazareth, whom you crucified but whom God raised from the dead, that this man stands before you healed. He is
>
> "the stone you builders rejected,
>   which has become the
>   capstone."
>   Acts 4:10–11

The Cornerstone

> So this is what the Sovereign LORD says:

> "See, I lay a stone in Zion,
>   a tested stone,
> a precious cornerstone for a sure
>   foundation;
>   the one who trusts will never be
>   dismayed."
>   Isaiah 28:16

This is the second Old Testament reference to a stone. Again, the New Testament reveals who this stone represents. It is Jesus Christ, as stated by Paul and Peter.

As it is written:

> "See, I lay in Zion a stone that
>   causes men to stumble
>   and a rock that makes them fall,
> and the one who trusts in him will
>   never be put to shame."
>   Romans 9:33

For in Scripture it says:

> "See, I lay a stone in Zion,
>   a chosen and precious
>   cornerstone,
> and the one who trusts in him
>   will never be put to shame."
> Now to you who believe, this stone is precious. But to those who do not believe,

> "The stone the builders rejected
>   has become the capstone."
>   1 Peter 2:6–7

It is safe to conclude that the stone in Daniel refers to Jesus Christ since the other two prophetic referrals to a stone in the Old Testament refer to Jesus Christ.

Now, back to the dream. There is a massive statue—head of gold, chest and arms of silver, stomach and upper legs of brass, lower legs of iron, feet of iron and clay. A stone, not cut with hands, breaks the feet and crushes the statue. The stone becomes a mountain and occupies the entire earth. What does the vision mean? All conservative scholars agree. It represents the rise and fall of human empires. It represents the coming of Jesus Christ, the living stone, to set up his kingdom upon the earth. However, when and how that happens is a matter of considerable debate and controversy.

The Coming of Jesus: How and When?

Virtually all Christians believe in the coming of Jesus Christ to set up his kingdom. However, we do not agree on the details of when or how he is coming. There are three basic interpretations centered around the word *millennial. Millennial* means one thousand years, and used in the context of apocalyptic literature, it refers to a reign of one thousand years—a period of peace, happiness, and joy. Although I confess my bias toward the premillennial viewpoint, I will present all three for our consideration.

The Amillennial Viewpoint

The amillennial viewpoint states that there will be no future earthly kingdom. Christ will not come to the earth to set up a kingdom in Jerusalem and rule. Rather, this dream represents the first coming of the Lord to die on the cross, to be buried, and to rise again. He came for the purpose of setting up his kingdom. His kingdom is not political; it does not involve the nations and empires of this world. Rather his kingdom is spiritual. The dream represents the coming of Jesus to establish his spiritual kingdom here on the earth.

That doesn't appear to be the thrust of verse 44, however.

> In the time of those kings, the God of heaven will set up a kingdom that will never be destroyed, nor will it be left to another people. It will crush all those kingdoms and bring them to an end, but it will itself endure forever.
>
> Daniel 2:44

To those who suggest the coming of the rock represents the first coming of Jesus Christ and the establishment of his spiritual kingdom, the question then is, "If that is true, then why do all of these political powers exist today?" Jesus in his first coming did not crush or do away with the kingdoms of this world. They still exist today. The clear implication of this dream is that Christ will bring earthly kingdoms to an end.

The Postmillennial Viewpoint

The postmillennial viewpoint states that Christ will return to the earth after a millennial period of peace and joy. (Thus the word *post*millennial.) The church will prepare the world for Christ's coming by introducing Christian values into the world's system. When this happens, the world will be prepared for Christ, and then he will return.

Jonathan Edwards believed that he was living during the days of the millennial kingdom. When the great revival and awakening swept New England, he was convinced that he was about to bring in the coming of Jesus Christ. Postmillennialism is based on this hypothesis, that the world will get better and better and that the church will have greater and more significant influence on the kingdoms of the world. Then Christ will come.

It appears from this passage, however, that things do not get better. They get worse—from the purity of gold, to silver, to bronze, to iron, to a loosely mixed coalition of clay and iron. It appears through the course of human history the kingdoms deteriorate. There is a downward spiral that is only interrupted by the coming of Jesus Christ. In fact, the observations of human history indicate that the influence of the church is lessening not increasing. The church of Jesus Christ is losing ground, not gaining ground.

The Premillennial Viewpoint

This is the interpretation to which I subscribe. It states that things in the world will continue to get worse until at last, Jesus comes to set up his kingdom. He will come prior to the millennium *(pre)* and usher in a one-thousand-year reign of peace. In Nebuchadnezzar's dream, Christ's coming is connected to the Roman Empire.

The legs of iron and the feet of clay and iron may represent two stages of influence for the Roman Empire. The first stage is of purity and strength. The second stage is the feet of clay and iron. It could represent a renewed coalition of individual people, individual nations, individual people groups, loosely formed in a political coalition similar to the Roman Empire as it existed centuries ago. Later, I will deal with the prophetic content of Daniel. However, let me warn against two extremes when it comes to the subject of biblical prophecy.

The first extreme is to ignore biblical prophecy altogether. Who cares about the future? Who cares about dreams? Who cares about gold, silver, bronze, iron, and clay? To choose this extreme, however, is to ignore a significant part of the Scriptures that deals with prophecy and things to come. You cannot simply ignore a part of the Bible.

The second extreme is to tie people, events, and dates to biblical prophecy. If you lived through the Second World War, you heard a lot about Bible prophecy. As Hitler marched into each new country, students of Scripture said, "There it is. It's happening! It's the revival and resurgence of the Roman Empire. Nothing like this has happened since the fall of the Roman Empire. Therefore Hitler or Mussolini must be the Antichrist. We are living at the end of the last days." It all looked at that moment in history as if it were really happening. Looking back, that was obviously not the preparation for the coming of Jesus Christ.

I have a book in my office entitled *88 Reasons Why Jesus Is Coming in 1988*. I think it was September of 1988 he was supposed to come. I received a lot of telephone calls and letters from people in Grand Rapids and around the country. "What do you think of that? Do you think we ought to prepare for that? Do you think we ought to sell our property? Do you think we ought to give up on everything and go witness because Jesus is coming in September? This guy said so!" Well he has now reevaluated, and he thinks it might be '90 or '91, or '92 or '93, or . . . He has totally discredited himself.

One extreme is to identify all the people, places, times, and dates. The other extreme is to ignore it. Are we living in the last days? I don't know. I tend to think so. Something dramatic is happening in Europe. It's called the European Common Market. It is a coalition of iron and clay. Individual countries and people groups are united in an economic and political coalition. Until recently the revival of the Roman Empire was impossible because Europe was Eastern Europe and Western Europe. Two separate coalitions with no possibility of unity. But the Berlin Wall fell overnight! All of Eastern Europe is now applying to join the Common Market. The pieces of the prophetic puzzle appear to be falling in place as never before since Jesus Christ ascended into heaven. Israel is back in the land, and when Jesus comes he will reign from Jerusalem. It presupposes a nation-state. The Roman Empire is being revived, at least in economic and cooperative terms. Daniel says, "One day when that coalition is in place, with iron and clay, a rock will intervene in the events of human history. Jesus Christ will return with glory and crush the kingdoms and powers of this world. They will beat their swords into plowshares, and Jesus Christ will sit upon the throne, and his kingdom will never pass away."

Insight

Given the disagreement among Christians over how to interpret the coming of Jesus Christ, there are nevertheless some common insights from this passage.

1. *God rules, and Christ is coming.* Whatever your interpretation of human history, two realities remain. God rules in human history, and Christ is coming.

First, God is the sovereign Lord of human history. Perhaps the clearest modern illustration of this is the fall of Communism. I was in Romania during the first free elections in that country after the fall of Communism. I met with some university students who told me, "Before the revolution, there was no God. After the revolution, there must be a God. Only God could make this happen."

Second, Christ is coming. The world is moving toward God's objective. There is hope beyond this life. Our hope is in Christ.

2. *Don't forget your friends.*

Then King Nebuchadnezzar fell prostrate before Daniel and paid him honor and ordered that an offering and incense be presented to him. The king said to Daniel, "Surely your God is the God of gods and the Lord of kings and a revealer of mysteries, for you were able to reveal this mystery."

Then the king placed Daniel in a high position and lavished many gifts on him. He made him ruler over the entire province of Babylon and placed him in charge of all its wise men. Moreover, at Daniel's request the king appointed Shadrach, Meshach and Abednego administrators over the province of Babylon, while Daniel himself remained at the royal court.

Daniel 2:46–49

After this powerful prophecy, this panoramic view of human history, and after the honor given to Daniel by the king (elevated to the highest position in the kingdom), Daniel does not forget his friends who prayed with him. They had interceded with him for the wisdom and direction of God. Now that Daniel is rewarded, he shares the honor with his friends.

Don't forget the people who pray for you. Don't forget the people who love you.

Prayer

Lord, I confess that my focus is almost entirely earthbound. I see through a glass darkly. Remind me that you are in control of history and that all of history is moving toward Christ's coming. Help me to live today with that reality in mind. Help me to speak, think, and act as if you were to come today. Amen.

Chapter Six

Standing Strong under Pressure

Daniel 3:1–30

In Michigan, whenever you think of fall you think of football. And whenever you think of football, you think of the University of Michigan and Michigan State. Unfortunately (or fortunately), I'm a Notre Dame football fan. When I came to Michigan years ago, I did not think that cheering for Notre Dame would be a problem. However, I discovered that most Michigan people cheer for the University of Michigan, or for Michigan State, or for whatever team is playing Notre Dame. To say that Notre Dame is not appreciated in Michigan would be an understatement of significant proportion. Every fall I get pressured to drop my allegiance to Notre Dame and *really* become a Michigander.

The story we are confronted with in the third chapter of Daniel is the story of three men who are under pressure to change teams. They are under pressure to forsake their loyalty to God and exchange it for religious loyalty to King Nebuchadnezzar. In the face of such pressure, they stand strong and loyal to God.

The Image of Gold

King Nebuchadnezzar made an image of gold, ninety feet high and nine feet wide, and set it up on the plain of Dura in the province of Babylon.

Daniel 3:1

59

In the previous chapter we discussed Nebuchadnezzar's dream and its interpretation. The dream was about a large statue. It had a head of pure gold, chest and arms of silver, stomach and upper legs of brass, lower legs of iron, and feet of iron and clay. The parts of the statue represent the rise and fall of world empires. Daniel tells Nebuchadnezzar that he is the head of gold. Daniel tells him, "The God of heaven has given you dominion and power and might and glory. . . . You are that head of gold" (Dan. 2:37–38).

Apparently this dream had captured the imagination of Nebuchadnezzar to the point where he decided to build a statue of gold. So about eighteen years after the dream, he launches a project to build a statue ninety feet high and nine feet wide. We do not know what the statue was like, but it was most likely a human being and perhaps the image of Nebuchadnezzar. The fact that it is not proportionate for a human being (90 ft. x 9 ft.) was not a problem for the Babylonians, since much of their art emphasized figures that to us seem grotesque and out of proportion. Nebuchadnezzar sets the statue up in the plain of Dura, which is approximately six miles southeast of the city of Babylon.

> He then summoned the satraps, prefects, governors, advisers, treasurers, judges, magistrates and all the other provincial officials to come to the dedication of the image he had set up. So the satraps, prefects, governors, advisers, treasurers, judges, magistrates and all the other provincial officials assembled for the dedication of the image that King Nebuchadnezzar had set up, and they stood before it.
>
> Daniel 3:2–3

He brings together the various officials of his empire.

- satraps—chief representatives of the king in each province
- prefects—military chiefs
- governors—government department heads
- treasurers—financial officers
- judges—guardians of the law (interpreted the law)
- provincial officials—assistants to the governors

While the text is not clear on Nebuchadnezzar's reason for building this statue or calling the officials of the empire together, it is likely he had two things in mind. First, he had a religious objective in mind. This may have been a religious act of worship to the Babylonian god Bel. Bel had given Nebuchadnezzar victory in all his battles. Second, Nebuchadnezzar may have had political reasons in mind. This act of worship may have been a litmus test of loyalty to the Babylonian Empire and to Nebuchadnezzar the king.

Strike Up the Band

> Then the herald loudly proclaimed, "This is what you are commanded to do, O peoples, nations and men of every language: As soon as you hear the sound of the horn, flute, zither, lyre, harp, pipes and all kinds of music, you must fall down and worship the image of gold that King Nebuchadnezzar has set up. Whoever does not fall down and worship will immediately be thrown into a blazing furnace."
>
> Daniel 3:4–6

This was quite a band. Note the broad diversity of musical instruments.

horn—horn of a beast
flute—reed instrument
zither—stringed instrument like a harp
lyre—a smaller version of the harp
harp—twenty-stringed instrument
pipes—wind instrument

After listing these various instruments, the writer adds one last phrase, "and all kinds of music." This may have been the first Woodstock in human history.

Before we continue with the story, there is a small technical problem we must address. The word used for *herald* in verse 4 is the word *karoz*, which comes from the Greek language. The Book of Daniel has always been the focus of attacks by liberal scholars who have sought to explain away the prophetic passages. In order to do that, they date the book much later than conservative scholars and then argue that the prophetic passages were actually written after the events took place—not before them. This removes the supernatural predictions of Daniel. Liberal scholars have pointed to this Greek origin of *herald* to promote the idea that Daniel was actually written in the late Greek or early Roman period of history. Therefore, the empires described in Nebuchadnezzar's dream in chapter 2 were actually written *after* the empires existed, not before. However, further study of ancient history has revealed that there was a strong Greek influence in Babylon long before Daniel arrived. Greek traders existed in Egypt and Asia in the seventh century before Christ. Greek mercenaries served in foreign armies—including the army of Nebuchadnezzar. So it would not be uncommon to see Greek influence in the language of Babylon.

Bow or Burn

> Whoever does not fall down and worship will immediately be thrown into a blazing furnace.
>
>   Daniel 3:6

The choice was clear. Bow down and worship or be thrown into a fiery furnace. The three Hebrews (Shadrach, Meshach, and Abednego) refuse to bow down, and the astrologers become upset. "At this time some astrologers came forward and denounced the Jews" (Dan. 3:8). The word *denounced* literally means "to eat their flesh." They were chewed up by their enemies. These enemies report them to Nebuchadnezzar and accuse them of three things. First, they are accused of paying no attention to the king. Second, they are accused of not serving Nebuchadnezzar's gods. Third, they are accused of not bowing down to the image of gold.

The heart of this issue involves bowing down and worshiping. For the Hebrew young men this is where they are willing to take a stand. The words in the text "bow down and worship" are similar ideas. To worship is to bow down; to bow down is to worship. It means to submit to a greater authority, bow before someone greater than yourself, or be obedient to someone. Worship is not an outward feeling or emotion—it is the inward yielding of the heart to God. These Hebrew young men understood precisely what the king wanted them to do. He wanted them to bow down and recognize him as the ultimate authority. As Hebrews, the only God they recognized was the God of Abraham, Isaac, and Jacob, not the god of Nebuchadnezzar.

You Don't Negotiate with the Enemy

Nebuchadnezzar does not receive the news of the Hebrew resistance with kindness or tolerance. The text says that he is "furious with rage" (Dan. 3:13). Now that is mad. Nebuchadnezzar instructs the Hebrews to fall down when the music plays. He gives them one more opportunity. But in giving them another opportunity, he raises the stakes. He says, "But if you do not worship it, you will be thrown immediately into a blazing furnace. Then what god will be able to rescue you from my hand?" Nebuchadnezzar makes it a contest of gods. The Hebrews' response is quick and uncompromising:

> Shadrach, Meshach and Abednego replied to the king, "O Nebuchadnezzar, we do not need to defend ourselves before you in this matter. If we are thrown into the blazing furnace, the God we serve is able to save us from it, and he will rescue us from your hand, O king. But even if he does not, we want you to know, O king, that we will not serve your gods or worship the image of gold you have set up."
>
> Daniel 3:16–18

The Hebrews make three important points.

1. *We do not need to defend ourselves before you in this matter.* There are some choices that demand no explanation. For the Hebrew young men, this is one of those choices. Right is right and wrong is wrong. No need to explain. Their choice is rooted in one of the fundamental principles of their commitment to God—the first and second commandments.

> You shall have no other gods before me.
>   You shall not make for yourself an idol in the form of anything in heaven above or on the earth beneath or in the waters below.
>
> Exodus 20:3–4

The Hebrews will not negotiate these laws, and they know that by obeying God and not Nebuchadnezzar, the love of God will surround and sustain them.

They had some other options, but they would not bend. They could have said, "Well, it's really not a religious act. All I'm doing is demonstrating my loyalty to the political kingdom of Nebuchadnezzar. It's really not a religious choice." Or they could have said, "What's one simple act of bowing down in contrast to a life of commitment to God? I mean I probably would be better off alive in the courts of Nebuchadnezzar to influence him than to die simply because I refuse to bow down." Or they could have said, "I'm bowing down on the outside, but I'm standing up on the inside." Or they could have said, "Let's just bow down, but God really knows our heart. God really knows our intent. We really don't mean anything by it. So let's bow down physically, but knowing in our hearts that God is God."

They had some options, but they dismissed them because God had said, "You shall have no other gods before me, and you shall not make any graven image—an image of gold, ninety feet high and nine feet wide. I am a jealous God, and if you keep my commandments, I will surround you with my love." In that moment of crisis they said, "Nebuchadnezzar, there are some choices for which there is no compromise. There are some issues that are not to be discussed or debated or adjusted. There are some choices that are either right or wrong, and this one happens to be one of those choices. Therefore, we will not defend ourselves, we will not explain to you. Our responsibility is to obey God."

2. *The God we serve is able to save us.* How did they know this? First, from their knowledge of Hebrew history. They knew what God had done for Abraham and Sarah, Isaac, Jacob, Joseph, Moses, Joshua, Deborah, David, and others. Second, they remembered what God had done for them. Remember the dream of Nebuchadnezzar (Dan. 2)? The wise men were unable to tell and interpret the dream. The king ordered them executed. When the king's soldiers came to kill Daniel, he asked for time. That night he gathered Shadrach, Meshach, and Abednego together, and they prayed to God. God revealed the dream to Daniel, who in turn told the king. Daniel and his friends were delivered from death and were promoted in the kingdom. God had delivered them from certain death before, and they knew he could do it again.

3. *But even if he does not . . . we will not serve your gods.* The Hebrews understood that God could intervene and save their lives, but he was not obligated to do it. Their refusal to bow down was not based on an absolute promise that God would save them from death. They knew he could and had one time earlier. But they made the choice and left the consequences up to God. If God delivered—great. If God did not deliver—great. In the first case, they would live. In the second case, they would be in paradise. In either case they were willing to accept the plan and will of God.

Hot Is Hot

> Then Nebuchadnezzar was furious with Shadrach, Meshach and Abed-
> nego, and his attitude toward them changed. He ordered the furnace heated
> seven times hotter than usual.
>
> Daniel 3:19

Have you ever noticed that when you get mad you say and do things
that do not make sense? This is what Nebuchadnezzar does. He is furious, and he does two things that are funny—in a strange sort of way. First,
he orders the furnace heated seven times hotter. He thinks, "I'm really
going to zap these guys. I'm really going to make them suffer. Heat up
the furnace seven times over." Now if he really wanted to make them
suffer because he was angry, he should have reduced the heat of the furnace to make the death prolonged and extremely painful. But he is so
mad he doesn't make sense. He heats it so hot, they're *not* going to suffer. Death is going to be instant.

The second funny thing he does is that he "commanded some of the
strongest soldiers in his army to tie up Shadrach, Meshach and Abednego and throw them into the blazing furnace" (Dan. 3:20). He ties them
up! Where are they going to go when they get in the furnace? Are they
really going to escape? The Aramaic text means he tied them up tightly
so they would not get loose. This is incomprehensible. He's going to
dump them in a fiery furnace heated seven times hotter than usual, and
he ties them up to make sure they don't get out. He's not making much
sense.

Walking with God through the Fire

> Then King Nebuchadnezzar leaped to his feet in amazement and asked
> his advisers, "Weren't there three men that we tied up and threw into the
> fire?"
>
> They replied, "Certainly, O king."
>
> He said, "Look! I see four men walking around in the fire, unbound
> and unharmed, and the fourth looks like a son of the gods."
>
> Daniel 3:24–25

There is an interesting mathematical formula in this story. The formula
is: $1 + 2 = 4$. Shadrach, that's the one, plus two other friends, Meshach

and Abednego, in the fire equals four people. And the fourth person is like a son of the gods. The law is this: When you walk through the fire, you need a couple of faithful friends and the Son of God. Remember that this week. When you walk through the fire and the storm, you desperately need a couple of faithful friends plus the Son of God: $1 + 2 = 4$.

Scholars disagree as to the identity of this fourth person. Some think this person was an angel, and others think he was the Son of God (KJV). I tend to think the latter. God walked with them and protected them.

> Nebuchadnezzar then approached the opening of the blazing furnace and shouted, "Shadrach, Meshach and Abednego, servants of the Most High God, come out! Come here!"
> So Shadrach, Meshach and Abednego came out of the fire, and the satraps, prefects, governors and royal advisers crowded around them. They saw that the fire had not harmed their bodies, nor was a hair of their heads singed; their robes were not scorched, and there was no smell of fire on them.
>
> Daniel 3:26–27

Nebuchadnezzar's response is typical of his emotional nature.

> "Therefore I decree that the people of any nation or language who say anything against the God of Shadrach, Meshach and Abednego be cut into pieces and their houses be turned into piles of rubble, for no other god can save in this way."
> Then the king promoted Shadrach, Meshach and Abednego in the province of Babylon.
>
> Daniel 3:29–30

Insight

1. *There are some issues that require no defense or negotiation.* All of life is making choices. But there are some choices that ought to be easy to make. These choices involve obedience to God. Now the consequences may be difficult to endure, but the essence of the choice is simple. Will I obey God or not? When we are faced with these choices, there is often the temptation to negotiate lesser options or explain and defend what we intend to do. Obedience to God cannot be negotiated, nor does it need to be defended.

I am a Baptist in my convictions about theology, the Bible, and the church. However, I serve in a church that is *non*-Baptist. It has a strong nondenominational tradition. When I first came to Calvary Church, many of my Baptist friends that I love in the ministry said, "How in the world could you go to a non-Baptist church?" Or, "How could you go to a church like that? You're walking away. You'll never be accepted again by Baptists. It simply means you really weren't a Baptist to begin with."

Initially I tried to defend myself, but then I realized there are some choices that require no defense. I simply responded, "I'm going to Calvary Church because that's where God wants me to go. My choice is simple, I either obey God, or I disobey him. If you don't happen to like the choice I've made, it's not my fault. You have to take it up with God."

Now in all of our lives we are compelled to make those kinds of choices. The pressure is always there to back off, to renegotiate, to adjust, to shift, to change. Thank God for Shadrach, Meshach, and Abednego, who stood before the king and said, "We're not even going to defend ourselves. We're not even going to explain it. We're not going to negotiate. We're not going to look at other options." When it comes to obedience to God it's either *yes* or *no*.

2. *We must obey God whatever the consequences.*

> But even if he does not, we want you to know, O king, that we will not serve your gods or worship the image of gold you have set up.
>
> Daniel 3:18

Their faith began with what God could do. They said, "We're not going to bow. We're not going to worship the image. Our God is fully capable of delivering us. He is able. He will deliver us from your hand." Their faith is in the power of God. But then their faith moves to the next level in the next verse. It moves from a faith in the power of God (what he can do) to a faith in the person of God (who he is). "Even if he does not deliver us, we are still going to trust him," they say.

I'm convinced most of us live on the first level of faith. Our trust in God and faith in God is very much connected to what God is going to do for us. We have a formula faith that says: "If I read the Bible, if I go to church, if I confess my sins, if I give money, if I get baptized, if I do all of the things that God wants me to do, *then* God will take care of all of my troubles and all of my problems and all of my difficulties." It's faith in what God can do.

But what about when God doesn't do what we think he ought to do? We know he is able. We know he is powerful. We know he can intervene. We know he can perform miracles, and we trust him. But what about those times when there are no miracles, when there is no intervention, when the circumstances of our lives defy logic and defy explanation?

As a pastor, I can tell you about all the times when the circumstances seemed hopeless. We prayed. God answered, and deliverance came. These were moments of unrestrained joy, thanksgiving, and celebration. But I can also tell you about times when the circumstances seemed hopeless. We prayed, and nothing happened. In fact, many times it got worse. I think of Vern. He and his family knelt at the altar of our church on a Sunday night. We prayed for the bone marrow transplant he was about to receive. The next time he came to the altar was a few weeks later—in a casket. And Vern's story is repeated over and over. Trusting God when he does *not* deliver requires a greater degree of maturity and faith.

As I have lived and prayed and wept with families like Vern's, I have learned that it is one thing to trust God who delivers, but it's an entirely different level of spiritual maturity to trust him when he doesn't deliver. When the pain is there and the hurt is there and the anger is there, it's tough to trust God. We know that our times are in God's hand. We know that all things work together for good from the perspective of God. But there are times in all of our lives where in the midst of the crisis, sitting in the darkness, it makes absolutely no sense! How could this work together for good? In our darkness we still must trust God, not for what he is able to do as much as for who he is. He has demonstrated himself through all of history as a God who is reliable and faithful and who can be trusted. These Hebrew young men demonstrate that level of maturity in their faith. They stand before Nebuchadnezzar and say, "Our God is able to deliver us; we have faith in his power. But we also know enough about God to know that we can still trust him when he chooses not to deliver."

3. *What are you willing to sacrifice for God?* Nebuchadnezzar makes an incredible statement about Shadrach, Meshach, and Abednego.

Then Nebuchadnezzar said, "Praise be to the God of Shadrach, Meshach and Abednego, who has sent his angel and rescued his servants! They

trusted in him and defied the king's command and were willing to give up
their lives rather than serve or worship any god except their own God."
                                                                    Daniel 3:28

They are "willing to give up their lives." What a profound statement. We
speak of Christian faith today in terms of what you can get. What God
will do for you. What Jesus will give to you. We speak of the advantages
of following Jesus Christ. It's called prosperity theology. If you believe
God, trust God, and follow God, God will give all of this stuff to you—
all of these blessings. Shadrach, Meshach, and Abednego are motivated
by what they are willing to give up for him—not what they want to get
from him. This is an important biblical principle.

> By faith Moses, when he had grown up, refused [he gave up something]
> to be known as the son of Pharaoh's daughter. He chose to be mistreated
> along with the people of God rather than to enjoy the pleasures of sin for
> a short time. He regarded disgrace for the sake of Christ as of greater value
> than the treasures of Egypt, because he was looking ahead to his reward.
>   Hebrews 11:24–26

In the Old Testament there is the story of King David. Moved with
pride, he takes a census of the people. He does it in disobedience to the
Lord. The prophet Gad comes to him and rebukes him saying, "Because
you disobeyed God you have three choices. One, three years of famine.
Two, three months fleeing from your enemies. Three, three days under
the plague." David chooses the latter. Repentance is brought about in his
life.

> On that day Gad went to David and said to him, "Go up and build an altar
> to the LORD on the threshing floor of Araunah the Jebusite."
>   2 Samuel 24:18

David goes up and tells Araunah what he wants to do. Araunah offers
him his property to build the altar. He does it without cost.

> But the king replied to Araunah, "No, I insist on paying you for it. [Notice
> this statement.] I will not sacrifice to the LORD my God burnt offerings
> that cost me nothing."
>   2 Samuel 24:24

"I will not accept it as a gift, because I will not offer to God something that cost me nothing," David says. I'm afraid that we are attempting to reduce our Christian faith to a cost-me-nothing faith and a give-up-nothing faith. But those who have stood for God in moments of crisis have been people like Shadrach, Meshach, Abednego, David, and Samuel who understood that following God costs something.

What are you giving up for God? What sacrifices are you making for the kingdom? What areas of your life demonstrate discipline and restraint? God has so blessed us that there is the tendency to worship at the altar of gold and materialism. Maybe you don't need a better car. Maybe, because God leads you to, you should give that up and give more money away. We live without restraint. We eat what we want—more than we need. We buy things that are unnecessary. We overindulge in our lives and claim to sacrifice for Jesus Christ.

4. *The will of God may take us through the fire.* Following God does not guarantee immunity from hardship or loss. In fact, it may well qualify us to suffer. God's will may take us through the fire.

> They preached the good news in that city and won a large number of disciples. Then they returned to Lystra, Iconium and Antioch, strengthening the disciples and encouraging them to remain true to the faith. "We must go through many hardships to enter the kingdom of God," they said.
> Acts 14:21–23

We must go through many hardships in order to enter the kingdom of God. It is the will of God that we encounter adversity, difficulty, pain, and suffering, because it is in the crucible of that suffering that our faith is tested. Not the faith in what God is able to do, but the faith that demands our trust in him for who he is, whether or not he delivers.

5. *God may not deliver us, but he will walk with us through the fire.* There is a lot of talking today that claims total victory for every Christian. "If you confess your sin," it claims, "and trust God, you will be wealthy and healthy. God will always deliver you from trouble!" **NOT! NOT! NOT**! You may go through the fire, but God will walk with you.

> But now, this is what the LORD
>   says—
> he who created you, O Jacob,
> he who formed you, O Israel:

"Fear not, for I have redeemed you;
    I have summoned you by name;
        you are mine.
When you pass through the waters,
    I will be with you;
and when you pass through the
        rivers,
    they will not sweep over you.
When you walk through the fire,
    you will not be burned;
    the flames will not set you ablaze.
For I am the LORD, your God,
    the Holy One of Israel, your
        Savior;
I give Egypt for your ransom,
    Cush and Seba in your stead."

                    Isaiah 43:1–3

Recently one of the single adults in our congregation wrote the following on the back of the bulletin.

Do you need me?
I am there.
You cannot see me, yet I am the light you see by.
You cannot hear me, though I speak through your voice.
You cannot feel me, yet I am the power at work in your hands.
I am at work though you do not understand my way.
I am at work though you do not recognize my works.
I am not strange visions nor mysteries.
Only in absolute stillness beyond self can you know me as I am, and then
but as a feeling and a faith, yet I am there.
When you need me, I am there.
When you feel most alone, I am there.
Even in your fear, I am there.
When you pray and when you do not pray, though your faith in me is
unsure,
my faith in you never waivers because I know you,
because I love you, because I am there.

                    Your Friend, Jesus

Prayer

Lord, my faith is weak. I tend to trust you for what you will do for me. Help me to begin trusting you for who you are—not what you can do. Help me to rest in the assurance of your presence in the fiery furnace. Thanks for walking with me. Amen.

Chapter Seven

Pride Comes before a Fall

Daniel 4:1–37

Suppose I could pour some coffee, sit down across the table from you, and ask you this question, "What is God doing in your life?" How would you answer? Suppose I further defined the question by asking, "What has God done in your life this last week?" What would you say?

If you would ask me this question, I would pull out my Spiritual Journal. It is the record of what God is doing in my life. It's the record of my own struggles—my pride, my sin, my disobedience. It's the record of what God is teaching me through his Word. It's the record of my prayers to God. It's the story of how God is working in my life and how I am changing.

In Daniel 4, we have a similar record written by Nebuchadnezzar. It's the story of what God did in his life.

King Nebuchadnezzar,
To the peoples, nations and men of every language, who live in all the world:
May you prosper greatly!
It is my pleasure to tell you about the miraculous signs and wonders that the Most High God has performed for me.
How great are his signs,
   how mighty his wonders!

> His kingdom is an eternal kingdom;
>   his dominion endures from
>   generation to generation.
>   Daniel 4:1–3

The word *signs* comes from an Aramaic word meaning "that which points something out." When used with reference to God, it is something that points out the existence and power of God. Nebuchadnezzar says, "I want to share with you events in my life that point to the existence and the power of God"—signs. The second word, *wonders*, means "that which surprises or astonishes someone." Nebuchadnezzar says, "Here's my testimony. I want to tell you about the things in my life that point to the existence and working of God in such a way that my response has been astonishment and amazement." Now what's God doing in your life or in my life that points out his existence and power in such a way that our human response is to stand back in amazement at what God is doing?

For a pagan king, Nebuchadnezzar sure had a handle on theology. He declares that God's kingdom is an "eternal kingdom, his dominion endures from generation to generation" (v. 3). God's kingdom is not confined to one moment in time and space. When we encounter difficulties and when things go wrong in our lives, we only feel the emotion of the moment. We only see the tragedy of what is happening in our life. But God's perspective is totally different. His kingdom is not confined to a single moment in time—it is eternal. Furthermore, his dominion endures from generation to generation. God's workings in human history are consistent. He doesn't deal with us differently than he did with our parents or our grandparents or our great-grandparents. He does not deal with us differently than the people of the New Testament or the people of the Old Testament. God's kingdom, God's rule, and God's dominion transcends all generations. He is consistent in his rule. He is consistent in his promises. He is consistent in his relationships. He is consistent in his expectation. He is consistent in his power. He is consistent in his authority. He is consistent in his covenants. He is consistent in his Word. He is consistent in his will. God's rule is the same. Why? Because God is the same yesterday, today, and forever. He remains the same.

Not Another Dream

> I, Nebuchadnezzar, was at home in my palace, contented and prosperous.
> I had a dream that made me afraid. As I was lying in my bed, the images
> and visions that passed through my mind terrified me. So I commanded
> that all the wise men of Babylon be brought before me to interpret the
> dream for me. When the magicians, enchanters, astrologers and diviners
> came, I told them the dream, but they could not interpret it for me. Finally,
> Daniel came into my presence and I told him the dream. (He is called Bel-
> teshazzar, after the name of my god, and the spirit of the holy gods is in
> him.)
>
> Daniel 4:4–8

Nebuchadnezzar is at home in his palace "contented and prosperous"
(v. 4). The word *contented* means at rest or free from apprehension and
fear. The word *prosperous* literally means "growing green." It is a word
used to describe the condition of trees and grain. Nebuchadnezzar is at
rest. He is free from fear and apprehension. He is sitting around "growing green" and being prosperous. Not a bad condition to endure. His peace
and prosperity are rudely interrupted by a dream that terrifies him (v. 5).
The wise men of Babylon are unable to interpret this dream (v. 7), so he
calls for Daniel (v. 8). Nebuchadnezzar recognizes the ability of Daniel
to interpret dreams.

> I said, "Belteshazzar, chief of the magicians, I know that the spirit of the
> holy gods is in you, and no mystery is too difficult for you. Here is my
> dream; interpret it for me."
>
> Daniel 4:9

The Dream

There are four parts to the dream of Nebuchadnezzar: the tree, the
messenger, the person, and the reason.

The Tree

This is a mammoth tree. It is taller than any modern building, and it
can be seen all over the earth. It is a healthy tree that provides food and
shelter for God's creatures.

The tree grew large and strong and its top touched the sky; it was visible to the ends of the earth. Its leaves were beautiful, its fruit abundant, and on it was food for all. Under it the beasts of the field found shelter, and the birds of the air lived in its branches; from it every creature was fed.

Daniel 4:11–12

The Messenger

A messenger from heaven appears and orders the tree cut down. The branches are stripped, and the animals and birds who found food and shelter in the tree are scattered. However, the roots and stump of the tree remain with a fence around them.

In the visions I saw while lying in my bed, I looked, and there before me was a messenger, a holy one, coming down from heaven. He called in a loud voice: "Cut down the tree and trim off its branches; strip off its leaves and scatter its fruit. Let the animals flee from under it and the birds from its branches. But let the stump and its roots, bound with iron and bronze, remain in the ground, in the grass of the field.

"Let him be drenched with the dew of heaven, and let him live with the animals among the plants of the earth."

Daniel 4:13–15

The Person

But let the stump and its roots, bound with iron and bronze, remain in the ground, in the grass of the field.

Let him be drenched with the dew of heaven, and let him live with the animals among the plants of the earth.

Daniel 4:15–16

Note the change in the text from *it* to *him*. Now the dream includes a person who will lose his mind. At this point we are not told who this person is.

The Reason

The decision is announced by messengers, the holy ones declare the verdict, so that the living may know that the Most High is sovereign over the kingdoms of men and gives them to anyone he wishes and sets over them the lowliest of men.

Daniel 4:17

The purpose of God in the events of this dream is to demonstrate that he is the "Most High" and he rules among the nations promoting whomever he will to positions of leadership.

Good News—Bad News

Daniel is now ready to interpret the dream, but it is a good news—bad news situation. The good news is that Daniel has the interpretation. The bad news is that the interpretation will negatively affect Nebuchadnezzar.

> Then Daniel (also called Belteshazzar) was greatly perplexed for a time, and his thoughts terrified him. So the king said, "Belteshazzar, do not let the dream or its meaning alarm you."
> Belteshazzar answered, "My lord, if only the dream applied to your enemies and its meaning to your adversaries!"
>
> Daniel 4:19

Daniel pauses. The word translated "time" could also be translated "one hour." Daniel hesitates for one hour before he delivers the interpretation. The tree represents King Nebuchadnezzar and his empire. A kingdom that has expanded across the civilized world and gives protection and food to people all over the earth. The angel is God's messenger. He will cut down the tree. God is going to intervene in the king's life, and God is going to humble him. He is going to lose his mind. He is going to go through a period of temporary insanity when what he says will make no sense. In fact, he will be driven from his palace. He will live in the open for seven years. Then, when he acknowledges that God reigns, he will be restored to his kingdom (see Dan. 4:20–26).

How would you like to deliver this message to King Nebuchadnezzar? He is an emotional roller coaster. Earlier, he built an image. He tells everybody to bow down or they'll get burned. Shadrach, Meshach, and Abednego refuse to bow down, and they end up in the furnace. God delivers them. So Nebuchadnezzar sends out a decree that no one can say anything bad against the God of Shadrach, Meshach, and Abednego. And if they do, their houses will be reduced to piles of rubble. Nebuchadnezzar is a person of extremes. He thinks nothing of wiping out families and people who are disloyal.

Daniel looks at the king and says, "O how I wish this applied to your enemies. God is going to come into your life. You are going to lose your ability to reason and think. You will be driven from the palace. You will wander out in the open for seven years. The day will come when you will acknowledge that God rules in the affairs of human history, and when you do, God will restore you to the throne."

Daniel's Footnote to His Interpretation

Therefore, O king, be pleased to accept my advice: Renounce your sins by doing what is right, and your wickedness by being kind to the oppressed. It may be that then your prosperity will continue.

Daniel 4:27

Renounce your sins. The word *renounce* means to tear away or break off. It is a description of repentance. Notice that the outward manifestation of repentance is "doing what is right" and "being kind to the oppressed." Daniel says, "King, you think that you are in control? God is about to teach you the lesson of your life. He is going to humble you. He will drive you from the throne for seven years until you acknowledge that he is God." Daniel also knows that the God who rules in heaven is pleased to respond to a broken and contrite heart, and Daniel says, "If you will renounce your wickedness and be kind to the oppressed, and if you will demonstrate your repentance through a changed life, maybe God in his mercy and forgiveness will extend your reign of prosperity."

Pride Comes before a Fall

All this happened to King Nebuchadnezzar. Twelve months later, as the king was walking on the roof of the royal palace of Babylon, he said, "Is not this the great Babylon I have built as the royal residence, by my mighty power and for the glory of my majesty?"

Daniel 4:28–30

Nebuchadnezzar's predicted demise does not happen immediately. Nor does Nebuchadnezzar repent. In fact, he is filled with pride and arrogance. He talks about his "mighty power" and "glory" and "majesty" (4:30). Now

Nebuchadnezzar has reason to boast. Nebuchadnezzar forged and built the city of Babylon with an outer wall. The wall was 87 feet wide and 350 feet high. That's about the width of a six-lane highway. Can you imagine that? The city had a hundred bronze gates. Ancient writers stated that when the sun would come up in the morning and the sun would set in the evening, those gates looked like liquid fire—set into a wall 350 feet high. The Euphrates River ran diagonally through the city. There were fifty temples through the city. The main gate was called Ishtar. A road one thousand yards wide went down from that gate into the city. On either side of the road there were decorations in painted enamel tile. Large paintings of 120 lions and 575 dragons decorated the beautiful roadway that led to the main temple. The Temple of Marduk was built in pyramid form. It was six hundred feet high—almost twice the height of the wall. At the top of that was a statue to the gods, forty-nine feet tall, surrounded by pure gold furniture weighing over sixty thousand pounds.

Nebuchadnezzar married Amytis, Princess of Media. He brought her to Babylon, and she didn't like it. It was too flat. She had grown up in the mountains of Media and just hated Babylon. So Nebuchadnezzar decided to do something about it. He decided to build her her own mountain inside of Babylon, called the Hanging Gardens of Babylon. He built it on terrace brick with courtyards, flowers, trees, and palms. They say that miles away from the city of Babylon the thing that impressed you was not the wall or the six-hundred-foot-high temple with the forty-nine foot statue on top of it, but rising beyond the walls of that city was the mountain built for Nebuchadnezzar's wife. Is it any wonder he says, "Is not this the great Babylon I have built as a royal residence, by my mighty power and for the glory of my majesty?" (see Dan. 4:30).

From Dream to Reality

The words were still on his lips when a voice came from heaven, "This is what is decreed for you, King Nebuchadnezzar: Your royal authority has been taken from you. You will be driven away from people and will live with the wild animals; you will eat grass like cattle. Seven times will pass by for you until you acknowledge that the Most High is sovereign over the kingdoms of men and gives them to anyone he wishes."

Immediately what had been said about Nebuchadnezzar was fulfilled. He was driven away from people and ate grass like cattle. His body was drenched with the dew of heaven until his hair grew like the feathers of an eagle and his nails like the claws of a bird.

Daniel 4:31–33

Can you imagine the contrast in lifestyle? This is downward mobility! From the royal residence and the hanging gardens, from behind a wall 350 feet high, the greatest and most powerful king is reduced to mental and emotional instability. Not for a day. Not for a week. Not for a month. But for seven long years. Away from his throne. Away from his kingdom. Away from his accomplishments. He finds himself humbled and alone.

> At the end of that time, I, Nebuchadnezzar, raised my eyes toward heaven, and my sanity was restored. Then I praised the Most High; I honored and glorified him who lives forever.

> His dominion is an eternal
>   dominion;
>   his kingdom endures from
>   generation to generation.
>   Daniel 4:34–35

Nebuchadnezzar learns three important lessons from these turbulent events.

1. *He learns about the dominion of God.* The dominion of God is his control over human events. The king learns that God does not surrender that control to anyone. God does *not* lose control. In addition, God does not change the rules. "His kingdom endures from generation to generation." He doesn't treat you any differently than he treats me. He does not treat those who have come before any differently than us. The way God deals with human beings is true to his character, according to his Word, and by his will. He never changes.

2. *He learns about the desire of God.* God does what he pleases with the powers of heaven and the peoples of earth. This does not mean that God is irrational. God is not on an emotional roller coaster. It simply means that God has a will. God has a purpose. God has a plan. And God accomplishes his will, purpose, and plan.

3. *He learns about the distance of God.* No one can hold back his hand or say to him, "What have you done?" The ways of God are often a mystery. We cannot fully understand them. Sometimes there is no answer to the questions, "What have you done?" or "Why have you done it?" In fact, God is not obligated to answer to us.

Having learned these lessons about God, Nebuchadnezzar concludes by praising God.

> Now I, Nebuchadnezzar, praise and exalt and glorify the King of heaven, because everything he does is right and all his ways are just. And those who walk in pride he is able to humble.
>
> Daniel 4:37

Insight

1. *Whatever draws me closer to God is always just and right.* Whatever God uses in my life to draw me closer to him is always right and always just, but it is not always pleasant. What Nebuchadnezzar went through was not pleasant. It was awful! Can you imagine how people talked about him? Can you imagine how they joked about him? Can you imagine, if he understood, how embarrassed he must have felt? For seven years wandering in the royal forest—that was not pleasant. But it was right and it was just because it was from God and it brought him into a closer personal relationship with God.

2. *God is looking for repentance.*

> Therefore, O king, be pleased to accept my advice: Renounce your sins by doing what is right, and your wickedness by being kind to the oppressed. It may be that then your prosperity will continue.
>
> Daniel 4:27

Repentance is demonstrated by a dramatic change in behavior. Repentance from sin means to "turn around." It means I am going in one direction in disobedience to the God who loves me. Repentance is coming to the point where I acknowledge my sin and my disobedience, and I not only ask for forgiveness, but I turn from that sin. The result is a new direction: I live by God's standards. It is the acknowledgment of sin. It is seeking forgiveness of that sin. It is determining to walk in newness of life. The Scripture speaks of various kinds of repentance.

National repentance:

> If my people, who are called by my name, will humble themselves and
> pray and seek my face and turn from their wicked ways, then will I hear
> from heaven and will forgive their sin and will heal their land.
>
> 2 Chronicles 7:14

It is appropriate for nations to repent of their sins. What is true of a nation
is true of other institutions, including the church. There must be times of
communal repentance. We must admit our sin and confess it. We must
also change our direction and behavior.

Personal repentance that leads to salvation:

> From that time on Jesus began to preach, "Repent, for the kingdom of
> heaven is near."
>
> Matthew 4:17

> Peter replied, "Repent and be baptized, every one of you, in the name of
> Jesus Christ for the forgiveness of your sins. And you will receive the gift
> of the Holy Spirit."
>
> Acts 2:38

> In the past God overlooked such ignorance, but now he commands all
> people everywhere to repent.
>
> Acts 17:30

We have come to a time in western evangelical theology where in some
circles we promote what I would call "a cheap grace." It simply says,
"Believe in Jesus. Ask God to forgive you, but don't worry about turning
from your sin." Just believe! That is not one of the central themes of the
gospel. Jesus said, "I have not come to call the righteous, but sinners to
repentance" (Luke 5:32). Those who have violated God's standards.
Those who have fallen short of God's holy standard of perfection. Jesus
said, "I have come to call sinners to repentance."

Salvation begins when I acknowledge my sin. I have offended a
holy God, and there is nothing I can do to merit his forgiveness. I turn
by faith to Jesus Christ and accept him as my personal Lord and Savior. Turning from my sin in repentance to God and allowing his Holy

Spirit to absolutely, dramatically transform my life. No repentance—
no salvation.

Personal repentance that leads to sanctification:

Godly sorrow brings repentance that leads to salvation and leaves no regret,
but worldly sorrow brings death. See what this godly sorrow has produced
in you: what earnestness, what eagerness to clear yourselves, what indig-
nation, what alarm, what longing, what concern, what readiness to see justice done. At every point you have proved yourselves to be innocent in
this matter.

2 Corinthians 7:10–11

Paul is writing to Christians who were not pleasing and following God.
He calls on them to repent. Repentance is an important activity in the life
of every believer. We *all* fail God and sin. Therefore, we must repent and
seek his forgiveness.

3. *Our lives are in the hands of God.* As a king, Nebuchadnezzar was
the most powerful individual in the ancient world. He was the most unique
military leader who ever lived. He was one of the most brilliant con-
querors and builders who ever lived. No one could stand before his might,
his power, his wealth, his wisdom, and his building ability. He was a tree
that encompassed the earth! It is incomprehensible to understand him in
twentieth-century context. The most powerful and wealthiest person in
the whole earth.

God says, "I want to teach you a lesson. You think you're big? You
think you're strong? You think your bank account is good? You think
you are at rest without fear and apprehension? You think that everything
you touch turns to gold? You really think you're somebody? I want to
teach you a simple lesson: There is one person who rules with absolute
power in the events of human history—and it's not you, Nebuchadnezzar. It's me. I want to teach you that the life of the most powerful individual on planet earth is not in your hands—it's in my hands."

The lesson is this: Your life does not belong to you. Your life belongs
to God. When I recognize that God rules in the events of human history,
I recognize that the God who rules in human history is the God who has
my life, my decisions, my future, my family, my possessions, my ability, and my talent in his hands. Our lives are in the hands of God. So when

you go out to live for Christ this week and something happens at the office that gets you all bent out of shape, remember, God is ruling in the events of your life, and your life is in his hands.

I want to give you an assignment to remember two letters. My background through my mother is Plymouth Brethren. They are called the "PB." Those are the two letters I want you to remember—*PB.*

P—God has a *plan* for your life. That's important to know. God has a plan for my life. He is the one who rules in the affairs of human history. He is the one who is individually involved in the lives of those who believe *and* those who don't. God has a plan for your life. Wherever you are, whatever circumstances you face, God has not forsaken you. God is not silent. Although you may not hear him, God is not ignoring you. Although you may feel in darkness, God is on the throne, and he has a plan for your life.

B—God's plan for your life is always in your *best* interest. It may not seem like that for the moment. Remember, we have a tendency to look at our lives at the moment. God looks at our lives from a kingdom point of view. His kingdom is eternal. He endures from generation to generation. God knows the beginning from the end. God's perspective is far beyond our moment, our struggle, and our darkness.

So, God has a plan for your life. You say, "But you don't know what I'm going through." God has a plan for your life, and God's plan is always in your best interest. So what do I do? I respond by yielding myself to his plan in my best interest knowing, maybe not by experience or feeling, but knowing, because he is God, he knows what he is doing. He rules in the affairs of our lives.

4. *Life does not consist of the things we accumulate or the projects we accomplish.* When you draw the bottom line to life and you add up the column, life does not consist of the things we accomplish or the projects we complete. Why? Because we are not in control. God is in control. I am not in control of my life. God is in control of my life.

Jesus tells the story of the farmer who says, "I'll pull down my barns, and I'll build bigger barns. I'll say to my soul, 'Eat drink and be merry, you have a lot laid aside for many years.'" God says, "You fool!" It is a foolish choice to assume that life is composed of things we accomplish and accumulate. God said, "You're foolish—tonight I require your soul" (see Luke 12:16–21).

Life does not consist of what we accumulate or what we accomplish. So where are you spending most of your time, energies, effort, creativity, and priorities? Where are we spending that time? Much of our time, unfortunately, is consumed by accumulating and accomplishing. Nebuchadnezzar, who had accumulated more than anyone else in his world and more than all of us combined and more than a hundred Donald Trumps, learned that life does not consist of all of the things we have accomplished and accumulated. All of these things can vanish overnight.

5. *The process we endure may not be pleasant, but God has a purpose (product) in mind.* The process we go through in life may not be pleasant, but God has an objective. He knows what he is doing. That does not lessen the pain. It does not take away the hurt. It is not a kind of pie-in-the-sky theology that ignores the harsh reality of disappointment and setbacks. It does not ignore broken relationships, hurt, pain, and loneliness. It in no way removes that, but it helps us understand as we go through that process. God has not forsaken us. There will be times when it seems he is silent. There will be times of overwhelming loneliness. But you can be sure in your loneliness, God's dominion is eternal. God has a plan for your life. God is taking you through a process because he has an objective in mind. What is that objective?

> And we know that in all things God works for the good of those who love him, who have been called according to his purpose. For those God foreknew he also predestined to be conformed to the likeness of his Son, that he might be the firstborn among many brothers.
>
> Romans 8:28–29

God's objective in the life of Ed Dobson is to cut off all the rough edges—and there are lots of them. Through his Word, through his Spirit, and through the circumstances of my life, God is shaping me into the image of Jesus Christ—and sometimes that is not a pleasant process. Sometimes it's very painful. But my confidence is this: While the process is not pleasant, God knows what he is doing. God is shaping me into the image of Christ and drawing me closer to him. Whatever brings me closer to God, even if it is loneliness, is right and just, because God is at work in my life.

6. *The ways of God cannot be fully understood by human beings.*

All the peoples of the earth
    are regarded as nothing.
He does as he pleases
    with the powers of heaven
    and the peoples of the
        earth.
No one can hold back his hand
or say to him: What have you
      done?
                Daniel 4:35

I don't like this principle, because I like to see the mathematical formula: $1 + 1 = 2$. I like to know that if you do A, B, C, and D, God will do E, F, and G. Sometimes with God $1 + 1 = 3$, and A, B, C, and D, does not mean E, F, and G. But if I understood the way of God, the will of God, the desire of God, and the workings of God, then I would be God. By the very definition of God, there is part of him that we cannot fathom or understand. Frankly, the longer I live, the more people I meet who are believers, the more I am convinced that there are many experiences of life for which there is no human and logical explanation.

"Now faith is being sure of what we hope for and certain of what we do not see" (Heb. 11:1). There is something about faith that requires us to trust God even though it is hard to get a handle on it and even though we do not understand. It is the substance (right now) of things that we ultimately hope for. It is the evidence of what we cannot see. So there is something about faith that demands that we walk where we cannot see and that we trust when it seems as if there is no hope. It is trusting God for who *he is*, not for what *he does*.

Because there are times when what he does cannot be understood, we are required to shift to a higher level of faith and say, "God, I know that you rule in the affairs of my life. I know you do what you will, and you have a plan for my life. I know your plan is best. But frankly, God, I don't understand what you are doing. So I will trust you in the process, knowing that you have an objective in mind to make me like Christ. While I cannot explain it, I will trust you. My hope is that you know what you are doing, and the evidence I have is that you are the same yesterday, today, and forever."

Prayer

Father, I admit that your ways are beyond my understanding, so I rest in the comfort that you are in control of my life. I yield to your plan because it is in my best interest. Draw me closer to you through this process, and make me more like Jesus Christ. Remove pride, arrogance, and an independent spirit. I confess these attitudes as sin, and I ask your forgiveness in Christ's name. Amen.

Chapter Eight

When God Crashes the Party

Daniel 5:1–31

For the first four chapters of the Book of Daniel, Nebuchadnezzar has been the central figure. He has been the center of attention as king of the Babylonian Empire. But notice chapter 5 begins by introducing us to another king. "King Belshazzar gave a great banquet for a thousand of his nobles and drank wine with them" (Dan. 5:1).

The events of chapter 5 occur seventy years after chapter 1. So Daniel is now in his mideighties. Nebuchadnezzar, who reigned for forty-three years, is dead. After his death, his son Evil-Morodach comes to the throne, but he is extremely erratic and unpredictable. Two years later he is assassinated, and Neriglisar comes to the throne and reigns for four years, then he dies. His son, Laborosoarchod, ascends the throne while he is still a child. He reigns nine months, and there is a plot within the palace. Laborosoarchod is assassinated, and in his place they put Nabonidus. He then reigns for the next seventeen years. He appoints his son Belshazzar as the coregent. Father and son together oversee all of the Babylonian Empire.

Let's Party

While change takes place in Babylon, new events are also emerging east of Babylon in Persia. In the year 556 B.C. Nabonidus becomes the king of the Babylonian Empire. Three years earlier in Persia to the east (modern-day Iran), Cyrus II came to power. After ten years in power, the seventh year of Nabonidus, Cyrus marches north and conquers Media and unites Persia and Media into a new threatening world power called the Medo-Persian Empire.

In the seventeenth year of the reign of Nabonidus, Cyrus marches west toward Babylon. City after city falls to his power and might. King Nabonidus decides that something must be done. So he gathers his army together and goes out to meet Cyrus. He is quickly defeated by Cyrus, and his army is scattered.

Meanwhile back in Babylon, Nabonidus's son Belshazzar throws a party. He invites a thousand nobles to the party and drinks wine with them (literally, "before them"). Sitting on an elevated platform in front of all these people, Belshazzar starts to get stoned. Belshazzar is either unaware of or deliberately ignores the desperate situation the city of Babylon faces. It is now the *only* city unconquered by the Medes and Persians. Maybe this party is designed to boost morale, or maybe it is to drown out the reality of what the people face.

The story continues, "While Belshazzar was drinking his wine" (Dan. 5:2). The verb in this sentence means to get drunk on wine. The king begins to feel the intoxicating effect of the wine and comes up with a bizarre idea.

> While Belshazzar was drinking his wine, he gave orders to bring in the gold and silver goblets that Nebuchadnezzar his father [ancestor] had taken from the temple in Jerusalem, so that the king and his nobles, his wives and his concubines might drink from them. So they brought in the gold goblets that had been taken from the temple of God in Jerusalem, and the king and his nobles, his wives and his concubines drank from them. As they drank the wine, they praised the gods of gold and silver, of bronze, iron, wood, and stone.
>
> Daniel 5:2–4

Babylonian culture lacked restraint. They overindulged in food. They overindulged in drink. They overindulged in sex. So the scene before us is not a very pleasant one. It's the ultimate party—food, drink, and sex.

Apparently what happened was that Belshazzar would stand and say, "I propose we sing to the god of gold." So they pour wine in the sacred vessels from the temple, and they drink to the god of gold. Then they sing to the god of gold. When they are through drinking and singing, the king then proposes that they sing to the god of silver. They pour wine again into the sacred vessels from Jerusalem, and they drink and sing to the god of silver. Then they drink and sing to the god of bronze. Then to the god of iron. Then to the god of wood. Then to the god of stone. Over and over they are drinking and singing. They are having fun, and they are worshiping the pagan deities.

At the height of the party, God intervenes with a message for Belshazzar and his nobles.

> Suddenly the fingers of a human hand appeared and wrote on the plaster of the wall, near the lampstand in the royal palace. The king watched the hand as it wrote. His face turned pale and he was so frightened that his knees knocked together and his legs gave way.
>
> Daniel 5:5–6

Most drawings of this scene have a human hand writing on the wall. The hand is detached from the wall. But this is not what happened. The text states that these fingers "appeared" (5:5). This verb literally means "to come out of." Fingers come out of the wall and begin to write a message on the plaster of the wall.

A plaster wall was not the normal style of architecture in the city of Babylon. Almost all of the walls of buildings contained paintings of the conquests of Nebuchadnezzar and the history of Babylonian civilization. A plain plaster wall would be rare. However, in excavations of the palace in ancient Babylon, archaeologists have discovered a large hall, fifty-five feet by one hundred and sixty-nine feet. There are no paintings or decorations on the walls. All the walls were plaster. Most scholars agree that this room is probably the location of Belshazzar's banquet.

Don't Ask Me

I remember when I took Hebrew in graduate school. We had classes on Monday, Tuesday, Thursday, and Friday. Every Tuesday we had an exam—written or oral. The problem with this schedule is that in the fall

Monday night is an important night—it's time for Monday Night Football. So every Monday night I would try to study Hebrew as I watched football. Not a good idea! I would come to class on Tuesday unprepared for the test. If the test was oral, I hoped the professor would not call on me. This is how the wise men felt about Belshazzar. "Don't ask me to interpret the writing," they thought.

> The king called out for the enchanters, astrologers and diviners to be brought and said to these wise men of Babylon, "Whoever reads this writing and tells me what it means will be clothed in purple and have a gold chain placed around his neck, and he will be made the third highest ruler in the kingdom."
> Then all the king's wise men came in, but they could not read the writing or tell the king what it meant.
>
> Daniel 5:7–8

On the surface, the reward that Belshazzar offers is quite impressive. Nabonidus is first in the kingdom. Belshazzar, the son of Nabonidus, is second. Whoever interprets these words will be made number three. However, it really is not much of an offer. Nabonidus and his army have already been crushed by the Medes and Persians. All the cities of the empire, except Babylon, are already conquered. The Medes and Persians are already surrounding Babylon. There is not much of a kingdom left, and by sunrise it will all be gone. Being third in this kingdom would be similar to being captain of the Titanic. It sounds good, but who in their right mind would want the honor?

> Then all the king's wise men came in, but they could not read the writing or tell the king what it meant. So King Belshazzar became even more terrified and his face grew more pale. His nobles were baffled.
>
> Daniel 5:8–9

The king is now desperate. No one is able to interpret the writing on the wall.

When All Else Fails, Call the Man of God

> The queen, hearing the voices of the king and his nobles, came into the banquet hall. "O king, live forever!" she said. "Don't be alarmed! Don't

look so pale! There is a man in your kingdom who has the spirit of the holy gods in him. In the time of your father he was found to have insight and intelligence and wisdom like that of the gods. King Nebuchadnezzar your father—your father the king, I say—appointed him chief of the magicians, enchanters, astrologers and diviners.

Daniel 5:10–11

They find Daniel and bring him to the banquet hall. After refusing the gifts from Belshazzar, he agrees to interpret the writing. Think for just a moment about how Daniel must have felt. He is old, mature, and seasoned. God has richly blessed his administration under Nebuchadnezzar. He has lived through the uncertain and erratic transitions of power—the assassinations and the palace plots. He is aware of the approaching Medo-Persian armies, and he is fully aware of what they are going to do. Now he is called into this banquet hall. He makes his way in and sees an incredible sight. Almost unreal! People frozen in time. Vessels on the table spilled over with wine dripping on the floor. The vessels from God's temple scattered on the floor and over the tables. The king shaking from head to toe. The light of candlesticks flashing against the back wall where there are unusual words. What did Daniel think?

Many years ago I preached a sermon on this story. I described Daniel as the type *A* aggressive personality. He marches into this banquet hall. He kicks aside the goblets. He pushes his way to the front. But I have since changed my mind. The vessels scattered in the banquet hall are the sacred vessels from the temple in Jerusalem. I would suspect that if they were lying on the floor, Daniel may have even bent over, picked them up, and gently set them on the table. I think his heart was grieved at what had been done to the sacred vessels. Now he stands before the king, as he had stood before Nebuchadnezzar, and delivers the message from God.

Some People Learn the Hard Way

Daniel begins his message with a brief history lesson from Belshazzar's grandfather—Nebuchadnezzar (Dan. 5:18–21). He describes the power and influence of Nebuchadnezzar:

All the peoples and nations and men of every language dreaded and feared him. Those the king wanted to put to death, he put to death; those he wanted to spare, he spared; those he wanted to promote, he promoted; and those he wanted to humble, he humbled.

Daniel 5:18

Daniel reminds Belshazzar that when Nebuchadnezzar became filled with pride, God intervened in his life and humbled him. He became insane for a lengthy period of time "until he acknowledged that the Most High God is sovereign over the kingdoms of men and sets over them anyone he wishes" (Dan. 5:21). Daniel then accuses Belshazzar of the same arrogance and pride and further condemns him because he knew what God had done to Nebuchadnezzar.

The Problem with Pride

But you his son, O Belshazzar, have not humbled yourself, though you knew all this.

Daniel 5:22

Belshazzar was not ignorant about the sovereign God. He "knew all this." He had known about what God had done to Nebuchadnezzar, but he chose to ignore the lesson of history.

Instead, you have set yourself up against the Lord of heaven. You had the goblets from his temple brought to you, and you and your nobles, your wives and your concubines drank wine from them. You praised the gods of silver and gold, of bronze, iron, wood and stone, which cannot see or hear or understand. But you did not honor the God who holds in his hand your life and all your ways.

Daniel 5:23

What is pride? Daniel defines it from the life of Belshazzar. "You have set yourself up against the Lord of heaven" (5:23). The word translated "set yourself up" means to boast, to elevate, or to lift up. This is what Belshazzar did. He boasted about himself. He elevated himself. He lifted himself up against the Lord. This arrogance and pride was manifest in three different areas.

1. *He made light of sacred things.*

> You had the goblets from his temple brought to you, and you and your
> nobles, your wives and your concubines drank wine from them.
>
> Daniel 5:23

These vessels were dedicated to the worship of the living and true God.
They were consecrated for holy purposes. Belshazzar had desecrated these
vessels and committed sacrilege. He made light of the sacred objects.

2. *He praised other gods.*

> You praised the gods of silver and gold, of bronze, iron, wood and stone,
> which cannot see or hear or understand.
>
> Daniel 5:23

Belshazzar not only refused to submit to the God of heaven, he worshiped
his own gods. These were gods shaped and formed by human hands.

3. *He did not honor the true God.*

> But you did not honor the God who holds in his hand your life and all your
> ways.
>
> Daniel 5:23

He failed to honor the God who really matters. The God who held his
life and times in his hand. The Creator and Sustainer of human life. The
one who truly rules in the affairs of the universe.

Pride Always Brings a Fall

This is the inscription that was written:

> MENE, MENE, TEKEL, PARSIN
> Daniel 5:25

Daniel now interprets these strange words for the king.

This is what these words mean:

> *Mene:* God has numbered
> the days of your reign and
> brought it to an end.

> *Tekel:* You have been
>   weighed on the scales
>   and found wanting.
> *Peres:* Your kingdom is
>   divided and given to the
>   Medes and Persians.
>   Daniel 5:26–28

Mene—numbered
Tekel—weighed (and found light)
Parsin—divided

The underlying message is that God is sovereign over the kingdoms of this world (see Dan. 5:21). The message is clearly stated in the strange words that appeared on the wall behind Belshazzar. God's sovereignty is seen in three ways.

1. *God is sovereign in the length of our days.* This is the message of the word *mene*. God holds our lives in his hand. He orders our ways. He demonstrates his sovereign rule in our lives in the length of our days. There are no guarantees for tomorrow. In fact, there are no guarantees for today. "Just as man is destined to die once, and after that to face judgment" (Heb. 9:27).

2. *God is sovereign in the quality of our days.* This is the meaning of the word *tekel*. God measures and weighs our days. First, he weighs our deeds.

> Do not keep talking so proudly
>   or let your mouth speak such
>   arrogance,
> for the Lord is a God who knows,
>   and by him deeds are weighed.
>   2 Samuel 2:3

There is nobody like God. Hannah warns in her prayer, "Don't be arrogant. Don't speak proudly, because the God who sits in heaven observes our lives. He knows everything about us. He takes all of our deeds and places them on his scale."

Suppose we had a video of your life for the last seven days—everything you did. We announce this Sunday morning in your church, through a unique development in modern technology, we are going to show the video. If you did that to me, I would either find the erase button or disappear forever! But God is watching us. He is sovereign. There is nothing I did in the last seven days that he did not see.

God knows. God is taking the events of my life and setting them on his scale. I am not removed from accountability for what I do. The God who created me, who numbers my days, who holds my life in his hands, is the God who is weighing the deeds of my life.

Second, God not only weighs our deeds, he also weighs our motives. "All a man's ways seem innocent to him, but motives are weighed by the LORD" (Prov. 16:2). God looks beyond our outward actions. He sees the hidden motives of our hearts. He knows why we do what we do. Nothing is hidden from God, and he weighs (judges) those motives.

3. *God is sovereign in the judgment of our days.* This is the message of the word *parsin.* After death, there is judgment (see Heb. 9:27). We must all stand before God. While we may escape the judgment of others, we cannot escape the judgment of God.

Belshazzar was about to learn all these lessons in one night.

> Then at Belshazzar's command, Daniel was clothed in purple, a gold chain was placed around his neck, and he was proclaimed the third highest ruler in the kingdom.
> That very night Belshazzar, king of the Babylonians, was slain, and Darius the Mede took over the kingdom, at the age of sixty-two.
>
> Daniel 5:29–31

Insight

1. *God's person must take a clear stand against the excesses of the culture.* Babylonian culture was a culture of excesses. They overindulged in food, wine, sex, and material things. There was little or no restraint. The story of Belshazzar is the story of that culture. It was the ultimate party—food, wine, and sex.

Daniel is a clear contrast to this lack of restraint. When he was a young man, he made some rather extreme choices that placed him at odds with the spirit of the Babylonians.

> But Daniel resolved not to defile himself with the royal food and wine, and he asked the chief official for permission not to defile himself this way.
>
> Daniel 1:8

To have eaten the royal food would have been clear disobedience to the Old Testament law. He would not do it because that meant disobedience to the law of God.

Notice that Daniel would not drink the wine. Now there was no law of God that required abstinence from wine. The law required moderation and restraint—not abstinence. Daniel makes an extreme choice. He says, "No, I will not accept the principle of moderation." He says, "I'm going to draw the line. I'm not going to eat the food because it's against God's law, nor am I even going to drink the wine." Why? I think the compelling reason that shaped his choice may have been as follows. Daniel understood that in Babylon wine abuse was a major problem. Daniel decides, "In a culture with no restraints, I'm going to be radically different. Call me extremist. Call me fanatical. Call me legalistic. Call me whatever you want, but I'm not going to drink wine." It was a statement against the excesses of the culture of that day.

There are clear similarities between Babylon and modern culture. We live in a culture of little restraint. We overindulge in food. We abuse alcohol. We live for pleasure and self-satisfaction. In the face of these excesses, the person of God is called upon to make radical choices of restraint and discipline.

2. Disobedience to God brings judgment. This is *not* popular theology today, but it is biblical theology. When I reject God's revelation and disobey him, I must face the judgment of God.

"But you his son, O Belshazzar, have not humbled yourself, though you knew all this" (Dan. 5:22). You know what Daniel is saying? "King, you knew what God wanted in your life. You knew that he desired humility and submission. He rules in your life and in the affairs of human history. You knew that! You saw it lived out in the life of Nebuchadnezzar. You had all of the information to make the right decision. But even though you knew it, you did not humble yourself. What's the result? Now you must suffer the judgment of God."

> Do not be deceived: God cannot be mocked. A man reaps what he sows. The one who sows to please his sinful nature, from that nature will reap destruction; the one who sows to please the Spirit, from the Spirit will reap eternal life.
>
> Galatians 6:7–8

> He who conceals his sins does not
>   prosper,
>   but whoever confesses and
>   renounces them finds
>   mercy.
>   Proverbs 28:13

When I look at my life and I understand what God wants in my life and I choose to ignore that, then judgment will follow. You see, most of us as Christians don't need any more preaching. We just need more obeying. We don't need a lot more insight. We simply need to respond with obedience to the insights God has already given us. There is always a warning. God is never mocked. When I choose to deliberately disobey him, I become the object of his judgment.

My prayer for Ed Dobson this week is simple: "God, I want to obey you. As you reveal areas of my life where I need obedience, I want to obey you." My second prayer is: "God, in a culture of no restraints, give me sensitivity and courage to take a clear stand and to demonstrate in my life that I am willing to be radically different."

3. *Dealing with pride is a lifelong struggle.* We have already noted that Belshazzar's pride was manifest in three areas: He made light of sacred things, he praised other gods, and he did not honor the true God. These are the same areas of pride in our own lives.

Making light of sacred things. In the Old Testament, the temple was the place where God chose to reside. Everything in the temple was holy and consecrated. It was uniquely set apart as sacred. To treat lightly the things of the temple was to trample on the holiness and sacredness of God, which is precisely what Belshazzar did. He took those vessels that were dedicated to God and treated them lightly. He trampled over them, and in so doing, he made light of sacred things.

In the New Testament, God is described as residing in the bodies of believers. These bodies become his temple, and this temple becomes holy and sacred.

> Flee from sexual immorality. All other sins a man commits are outside his body, but he who sins sexually sins against his own body.
>   1 Corinthians 6:18

My body belongs to God. My body is the dwelling place of God. Therefore, it is important that I treat it accordingly.

> Don't you know that you yourselves are God's temple and that God's Spirit lives in you? If anyone destroys God's temple, God will destroy him; for God's temple is sacred, and you are that temple.
>
> 1 Corinthians 3:16–17

Serving other gods. Anything that I love, serve, or worship more than God is a god. It can be a sport or a sports car. It can be a job or a house. It can be a hobby. Anything that comes between me and God is a god. And serving other gods only brings the judgment of the true and living God.

Failing to honor God. This is where many Christians stumble. We like to honor ourselves. We take the honor for our own ability. We take the honor for our own accomplishments. We are impressed when others recognize us. We like it when others affirm us. When I take the honor for myself, I rob God of his honor, and I am manifesting pride in my life.

So what do I do about this struggle with pride? Number one, whenever I am desecrating my body, making light of sacred things, or failing to give God all of the honor, I must acknowledge that I struggle with pride. Be honest and admit the problem to God. The problem is my own desire to be important and to be the center of attention. The problem is me!

Step number two, confess pride as sin. It is the sin that caused the fall of Satan. Read Isaiah 14:12–15. It's pride that plunged the human race into sin. Pride! We like to talk about all sorts of other sins, but we don't like to talk about pride, because pride hits us where we are living.

Step number three, start to serve others.

> Therefore, O king, be pleased to accept my advice: Renounce your sins by doing what is right, and your wickedness by being kind to the oppressed. It may be that then your prosperity will continue.
>
> Daniel 4:27

You know how to overcome pride. You make a commitment to serve others. In this context, the most oppressed and forsaken of all. You don't try to be humble, because then you become proud in your humility. The only way to overcome pride, Jesus said, is to be the servant of all. So, when you go to the office this week, don't order anybody to make the coffee. Do it yourself and serve everybody else. Ask God to help you see those who are oppressed and those who are hurting. In the love of Jesus Christ, serve them. It is in the service of others that we discover what genuine humility is all about. And it is in the service of others that God delivers us from pride.

Prayer

Lord, I am surrounded by the temptations of the flesh. There is little restraint in pleasure, eating, and drinking. Give me the courage to be different. I yield my body to you and to the disciplined control of your Holy Spirit. Help me not to be seduced by the neon signs of a culture gone bad. Amen.

Chapter Nine

Taking a Stand for God in the Marketplace

Even if it means being thrown to the lions

Daniel 6:1–28

The story of Daniel in the den of lions is one of the most familiar stories in the Bible. It is one of those stories that children learn at an early age. Yet beneath the surface of this exciting story there are some important lessons to learn. Lessons about prayer. Lessons about faith. Lessons about courage. Lessons about taking a stand for God even when it might cost you your life.

Daniel's Promotion

It pleased Darius to appoint 120 satraps to rule throughout the kingdom, with three administrators over them, one of whom was Daniel.

Daniel 6:1–2

Darius is the governor of Babylon. He answers to Cyrus, the emperor, who had conquered the Babylonian Empire. Darius begins by reorganizing the political structure. He appoints 120 satraps. Satraps were department heads or administrators. He then appoints three chief administrators. Each of the 120 satraps answers to one of these three administrators.

Daniel's Integrity

As an administrator, Daniel excels to the point where Darius wants to put him over the entire kingdom (see Dan. 6:3). He wants to appoint Daniel as the chief of staff. This potential appointment is not received well by the other two administrators and the satraps. However, they could find no substantive basis on which to discredit Daniel so that Darius would not appoint him as chief of staff.

> At this, the administrators and the satraps tried to find grounds for charges against Daniel in his conduct of government affairs, but they were unable to do so. They could find no corruption in him, because he was trustworthy and neither corrupt nor negligent.
>
> Daniel 6:4

The text states that they "could find no corruption in him" (v. 4). What a statement. These were people who observed Daniel's life in the marketplace every day. They sat in meetings with him. They talked through decisions together. They took orders from him. And they could find no corruption. In fact, Daniel possesses three qualities that elevate him above political corruption.

1. *He is trustworthy.* The word used here means "to rely on" someone. You can depend on Daniel. He is a person of his word. He does not change with the shifting winds of political expedience. He does not change with the changing expectations of the palace or the people. He has *integrity*.

2. *He is not corrupt.* This word speaks of honesty. He does not lie. He does not steal. He does not manipulate. He does not abuse people. He governs with a consistent set of moral values that cannot be corrupted. Money, power, and sex do not rule his life. He has *honesty*.

3. *He is not negligent.* This word speaks of *industry*. He performs his duties with excellence. He works hard. He pays attention to all the details.

It appears from this story that not everyone in the political system demonstrates these qualities. But Daniel does. These are vital qualities for living out your faith in the marketplace. INTEGRITY. HONESTY.

INDUSTRY. Daniel's opponents have a problem. They cannot find a flaw in Daniel's character by which to discredit him—with one exception! His commitment to God.

> Finally these men said, "We will never find any basis for charges against this man Daniel unless it has something to do with the law of his God."
>
> Daniel 6:5

How do they know about Daniel's commitment to the law of his God? How do they arrive at that strategy? What causes them to conclude that the only ground for making a charge against Daniel is in regard to the law of his God? Reason number one, Daniel's commitment to God is public. That's how they knew! How do they know Daniel observes the law of his God? Because Daniel's commitment to God, to his Word, and to his law is not secretive. It is not something practiced behind closed doors or in the privacy of his own heart. Daniel is public. He takes a public stand for God. This stand is consistent for over seventy years—through Nebuchadnezzar, Belshazzar, and now Darius. Through the shifting tides of government bureaucracy and through the rise and fall of kingdoms and empires, Daniel remains uniquely consistent. He is committed to the law of his God, and he does not hide his commitment. They know because Daniel is publicly committed to God.

Number two, they devise this strategy because they not only know of his public commitment, but they understand the depth and strength of that commitment. These guys are talking about death. They want Daniel assassinated. They understand that there are some things that Daniel is willing to die for. And one of them is his commitment to the law of his God. What a remarkable testimony! Not a preacher. Not a theologian. Rather, a civil servant. A business administrator. A politician. He has a public commitment to God, and people know he would rather die than give up on his commitment to God.

Let's Make a Deal

> So the administrators and the satraps went as a group to the king and said: "O King Darius, live forever! The royal administrators, prefects, satraps, advisers and governors have all agreed that the king should issue an edict and enforce the decree that anyone who prays to any god or man during

the next thirty days, except to you, O king, shall be thrown into the lions' den. Now, O king, issue the decree and put it in writing so that it cannot be altered—in accordance with the laws of the Medes and Persians, which cannot be repealed."

                                                                    Daniel 6:6–8

This is a brilliant strategy. King Darius is suffering from the syndrome of being the senior vice president, not the CEO. He's not the one who is ultimately in command. He's second in command. Those of us who have served or are serving in subordinate roles can relate to the feelings that Darius must have had. You get none of the credit, right? But lots of blame, right? The person sitting in the big chair gets all the credit, all the benefits, all the affirmation. When presentations are made that you have worked on and developed, the boss is applauded. It is frustrating, at times, being the second in command. You do not have control. You are not in charge. You do catch a lot of the flack.

So they come to Darius, who's the senior vice president, and say, "Darius, do we have a plan!" And they appeal directly to his pride. You see, the king of the entire empire was considered the earthly representative of the gods. Nebuchadnezzar was the human representative of the great Babylonian god. Cyrus, the Persian, who is now the emperor, is considered by his subjects as the earthly representative of god. You worship him. You bow down to him. You pray to him. You honor him. You praise him—he's god!

So they come to Darius, who's probably frustrated because he's second in command, and they say, "I tell you what. Let's do a unique experiment for thirty days. Anyone in your province governed by the 120 princes who prays to anyone (God or man) other than you will be thrown into the lions' den." Can you imagine how that made him feel? He is allowed to sit in the "big seat" for thirty days. "You will be the god. You will be the earthly representative of the great gods, and the people will pray to you." "Great," he says. And he signs on to the plan.

When You Cannot Pray—You Had Better Pray

Now when Daniel learned that the decree had been published, he went home to his upstairs room where the windows opened toward Jerusalem.

Three times a day he got down on his knees and prayed, giving thanks to
his God, just as he had done before.

Daniel 6:10

Part of administration is the art of negotiation. Undoubtedly, Daniel
was a master at this art form. It's the ability to take two opposing positions and come up with an acceptable alternative. It's the ability to take
two groups or ideas that are mutually exclusive and bring compromise
so that both parties win. If ever Daniel needed negotiating skills, it was
now. Should he pray publicly or not? He has at least two options. First,
he could suspend all personal prayer for thirty days. After all, God would
understand. Or, in the second place, he could pray privately, and no one
would know the difference. Whether or not Daniel even considered these
options, we do not know. We do know that he continued his pattern of
prayer.

I am impressed by the fact that Daniel gets down on his knees to pray.
This is an act of humility. Remember, Daniel has a lot of qualities that
would tend to make one proud. He is intelligent. He is good-looking. He
is superior in wisdom and knowledge. He is a confident administrator.
He has integrity, industry, honesty, morality, and ethics. He understands
dreams and visions. He is the chief administrator. He has all sorts of abilities and skills that are admirable and desirable. How does a person like
Daniel stay humble? He has ability, skill, and wisdom. He is multilin-
gual. He understands Babylon. He understands Persia. He understands
Jerusalem. He understands God. He understands politics. How does a
person with all of those skills and abilities not become proud? The anti-
dote for Daniel is prayer. Three times a day he gets down on his knees
and recognizes his complete dependence upon God.

One of the ultimate acts of pride is prayerlessness. It says, "I don't
need you, God. I don't need your help. I don't need your wisdom. I don't
need your insight. I have all of the human abilities. I have all of the intel-
lect that I need. I have all of the reasoning powers that I need. I can do it
on my own."

Daniel is a unique individual who could have done it on his own, but
he has a practice—three times a day he leaves the affairs of state and gets
down on his knees to pray. Daniel prays.

The text reveals to us a number of elements in regard to prayer (Dan.
6:10).

1. the place of prayer—"his upstairs room"
2. the time of prayer—"three times a day"
3. the posture of prayer—"he got down on his knees"
4. the praise of prayer—"giving thanks to his God"
5. the request of prayer—"asking God for help" (6:11)
6. the habit of prayer—"as he had done before"

This Ain't Motel 6

Then they said to the king, "Daniel, who is one of the exiles from Judah, pays no attention to you, O king, or to the decree you put in writing. He still prays three times a day." When the king heard this, he was greatly distressed; he was determined to rescue Daniel and made every effort until sundown to save him.

Daniel 6:13–14

The opponents of Daniel report his praying to the king. The king is distressed when he finds out that it is Daniel who must be thrown into the lions' den. The king does his best to get around the decree and save Daniel's life, but he is unable to because of the legal system of the Medes and Persians (see Dan. 6:15). Daniel is taken and thrown in the lions' den.

In ancient days lions' dens were huge caverns in the ground. You could look down into them. In fact, most of them had a wall around the top about three feet high. Caverns were usually divided into two sections by a middle wall that had a door. The lion keeper was able to raise or lower the door from above. He would throw meat into one side of the cavern and then raise the door. The lions would go through, and the keeper would shut the door. He could then go down into the one side and clean it. There was usually an opening at one end of the cavern at ground level so that animals could be put in or taken out.

So the king gave the order, and they brought Daniel and threw him into the lions' den. The king said to Daniel, "May your God, whom you serve continually, rescue you!"

Daniel 6:16

Here is what the king is saying, "I have done all that I can within my power and by my authority to rescue you from death. There is nothing else that I can do."

The Faithfulness of God

Darius has a lot of love and admiration for Daniel. After Daniel is put in the lions' den, the king goes home to the palace. But he cannot sleep. He does not eat. He does not feel like being entertained (see Dan. 6:18).

> At the first light of dawn, the king got up and hurried to the lions' den. When he came near the den, he called to Daniel in an anguished voice, "Daniel, servant of the living God, has your God, whom you serve continually, been able to rescue you from the lions?"
>
> Daniel 6:19–20

Daniel responds to the anguished cry of the king.

> Daniel answered, "O king, live forever! My God sent his angel, and he shut the mouths of the lions. They have not hurt me, because I was found innocent in his sight. Nor have I ever done any wrong before you, O king."
>
> Daniel 6:21–22

Daniel credits the angel of God with saving his life. The statement suggests something that really does not make sense to a rational, logical mind. It is foolish to those who live each day by what they can see, what they can feel, and what they can touch. The Scriptures tell us that beyond the material world that we see and observe, there is a larger dimension called the spiritual world. Satan and his demons are alive in that world. Paul says we don't wrestle against principalities and powers (the authorities that we can see), but we wrestle against spiritual darkness (see Eph. 6:12). If you read the Scriptures, you know that Satan and his host of demons are alive and involved on planet earth. In that spiritual world God is also alive. God's army, called angels, are very much involved in the affairs of this world. "Are not all angels ministering spirits sent to serve those who will inherit salvation?" (Heb. 1:14).

Angels are sent to minister to us. A recent "Dennis the Menace" cartoon illustrates this point. Dennis has bruises all over him. His shirt is torn. His pants are torn. He has one shoe off and one shoe on. He is crying. He has a cut on his face with a Band-Aid on it. Sweat is pouring off him. He asks: "Do guardian angels take days off?" That's pretty good. The answer to that question is "No!"

God sent his angel into that lions' den, closed the mouths of the lions, and delivered Daniel. Perhaps Daniel was aware of God's promises in this regard.

> The angel of the LORD encamps
>   around those who fear him,
>   and he delivers them.
> > > > Psalm 34:7

> For he will command his angels
>   concerning you
>   to guard you in all your ways.
> > > > Psalm 91:11

The King Is Happy

Darius is delighted that Daniel has been spared. To celebrate this happy occasion, Darius does two things.

1. *He destroys Daniel's enemies.*

At the king's command, the men who had falsely accused Daniel were brought in and thrown into the lions' den, along with their wives and children. And before they reached the floor of the den, the lions overpowered them and crushed all their bones.

> > > > Daniel 6:24

2. *He decrees that Daniel's God must be feared and reverenced.*

I issue a decree that in every part of my kingdom people must fear and reverence the God of Daniel.
For he is the living God
    and he endures forever;
his kingdom will not be destroyed,
    his dominion will never end.
He rescues and he saves;
    he performs signs and wonders
    in the heavens and on the earth.
He has rescued Daniel
    from the power of the lions.

> > > > Daniel 6:26–27

Insight

1. *Integrity is critical in the marketplace.* Daniel's enemies could find no ground for a charge against him in his conduct or government affairs. He is trustworthy. He is not corrupt. He is not negligent. He has integrity.

Sometimes we get the idea that our religion belongs in one world and our work belongs in another world. We come to church on Sunday. We listen to the Word. We sing the songs. We worship God. We put money in the offering plate. We have this religious experience on Sunday. Then we walk out of the building to our office on Monday morning, and it's a different world there. Too often Christians are the ones who lack integrity. They lie. They cheat. They steal. They manipulate. They take advantage of people. They oppress people. They lack integrity. You can't rely on them. They are not honest in what they say, do, and promise. They are not industrious. They do not work hard. They get by with the least they can do. They do not take care of the details. They live whatever way they want the rest of the week. But they're Christians! When Sunday comes, they put on the same business suit in which they had lied, cheated, and stolen all week long, and they come to church carrying a Bible. They read from the Bible. They pray. They sing. They worship. They do their little Christian deal, and then they walk right back out into the world and live like the devil.

You know what Daniel is teaching us? You don't delineate a little religious world over here and the real world over there. To be committed to Christ, to God, and his Word encompasses all of the relationships in life. Daniel is a living testimony of what it means to serve God under unbelievable pressure and in a critical situation with integrity, honesty, and industry.

2. *Prayer is not optional.* Daniel is willing to die for prayer. When it came to choosing prayer and death or no prayer and life, Daniel chooses prayer and death. This suggests that for Daniel, prayer has a high level of value. He is willing to die for it. You can tell what is of ultimate value by what people are willing to die for.

I would give up my life to save my wife, because I value her love, friendship, and commitment very deeply. I would gladly give up my life for her or for any of my children. It would be an immediate, without discussion, decision. I value them to the level that is beyond money and beyond time. I value them, and I would be willing to give up my life for their benefit. That's the ultimate statement of value.

Daniel is willing to die for prayer. Think about that! Daniel is willing to give up his life to keep on praying. You know what that tells me? Prayer is important. Prayer has a high value in God's value system.

What is valuable to you? For most of us it's not prayer. It really is not. We would not die for it. You say, "Well, I would." But are you living for it? Are you making the sacrifices now? Are we on our knees praying to God? To live and not pray is not an option. Prayer unlocks power. It acknowledges our dependence upon God, and it is not optional—it is absolutely critical!

3. *How much of God can other people see in my life?* Notice the words I have italicized in the following verses from this story of Daniel.

> So the king gave the order, and they brought Daniel and threw him into the lions' den. The king said to Daniel, "May *your God*, whom you serve continually, rescue you!"
>
> Daniel 6:16

> When he came near the den, he called to Daniel in an anguished voice, "Daniel, servant of the living God, has *your God*, whom you serve continually, been able to rescue you from the lions?"
>
> Daniel 6:20

> The king was overjoyed and gave orders to lift Daniel out of the den. And when Daniel was lifted from the den, no wound was found on him, because he had trusted in *his God*.
>
> Daniel 6:23

> I issue a decree that in every part of my kingdom people must fear and reverence the *God of Daniel*.
>
> Daniel 6:26

The focus in these verses is the God of Daniel. The king sends out a decree in which he describes the God of Daniel. It is a profound statement of theology. Where did the king learn about the God of Daniel? He did not learn about him in Sunday school. He did not learn about him in a synagogue or church. He did not learn about him in a book of theology. He did not learn about him in the Scriptures. He did not learn about Daniel's

God the way most of us have learned about God—by going to church, by reading the Bible, by learning catechism, by attending Sunday school, by going to Bible studies, by reading books, or by studying theology. Darius learned about God as he saw God lived out in the life of Daniel.

Think about that! Everything Darius knew about God he learned by observing Daniel and his behavior. How much of God do other people see in the life of Ed Dobson? How much of God do your neighbors see in your life? What kind of a letter would be written about the God other people see in my life? Darius observed two compelling facts about the God he saw in Daniel's life.

He is a living God:

> For he is the living God
>   and he endures forever:
> his kindgom will not be destroyed,
>   his dominion will never end.
>   Daniel 6:26

I am afraid that for most of us, God is a series of theological propositions. God is spirit. God is holy. God is omnipotent. God is omnipresent. God is omniscient. God is mercy. God is love. We have all of these statements that describe God. We have a Bible that reveals to us the mind of God, the heart of God, the will of God, the character of God, the attributes of God, and the promises of God. We open our Bible, and we examine it. We look at it, we read it, and we draw conclusions about God. But I'm afraid that sometimes our definition of God is like this book. It is theory. It is theology. It is sentences. It is description. We have a tendency to confine God to the pages of this book.

Did you know that the same God who is described in this book is alive today? Did you know that? He is not dead! He is very much alive!

Darius said, "I know about the God of Daniel. He is alive. He exists. He is real!" I'm afraid that most of us have a going-to-church kind of God. He is a God of theological statements, not a God who is alive in our daily experiences.

The God who is alive is also involved in the events of life:

> He *rescues* and he *saves*;
>   he *performs* signs and wonders

in the heavens and on the earth.
He has *rescued* Daniel
   from the power of the lions.
      Daniel 6:27, italics added

Notice the verbs that define God's activity:

   he rescues
   he saves
   he performs signs and wonders

Darius knew that the God of Daniel was involved in human events because he saw that God delivered Daniel. Can others see a living *and* working God in my life? This ought to be the distinguishing feature of the people of God.

The LORD replied, "My Presence will go with you, and I will give you rest."
   Then Moses said to him, "If your Presence does not go with us, do not send us up from here."
                                                      Exodus 33:14–15

What distinguishes us from the rest of the people on the earth? What distinguishes us as a community of faith? Moses said that the distinguishing feature is that God himself goes with us. What kind of God is manifest in our lives? What evidence is there that God is alive and at work in my life? What kind of a God do others see in my life?

Prayer

Dear Lord, forgive me for my prayerlessness. My focus has been to ignore prayer—not value it. Forgive me and teach me to be like Daniel— three times a day on my knees in your presence. Amen.

Chapter Ten

Learning to Pray Like Daniel

Daniel 9:1–23

As we continue our study of the Book of Daniel, we move to chapter 9 (chapters 7 and 8 are addressed later in part 2). For those who are dispensational in their eschatology, Daniel 9 is one of the most significant prophetic passages in the Bible. This prophetic section is contained in the last four verses of that chapter. However, the first twenty-three verses are devoted to prayer. Daniel's prayer gives us practical insight into his method of prayer. We know that prayer is important to Daniel. It is so important that he was willing to die rather than stop praying (Dan. 6). As we examine this prayer of Daniel, we will discover nine characteristics of prayer.

Prayer Is My Response to God's Word

In the first year of Darius son of Xerxes (a Mede by descent), who was made ruler over the Babylonian kingdom—in the first year of his reign, I, Daniel, understood from the Scriptures, according to the word of the LORD given to Jeremiah the prophet, that the desolation of Jerusalem would last seventy years.

Daniel 9:1–2

113

Daniel was a teenager when the mighty armies of Babylon marched against Jerusalem. Daniel, along with several other young people from Israel, was taken captive and moved to Babylon. During that same period of time, the prophet Jeremiah had a ministry in Jerusalem. It was not a pleasant ministry. It was not a popular ministry, and it was not widely accepted. Jeremiah made some predictions about Israel's captivity.

> This is what the LORD says: "When seventy years are completed for Baby-
> lon, I will come to you and fulfill my gracious promise to bring you back
> to this place. For I know the plans I have for you," declares the LORD,
> "plans to prosper you and not to harm you, plans to give you hope and a
> future."
>
> Jeremiah 29:10–11

Daniel is now an old man. Somehow he has access to the writings of Jeremiah and discovers these incredible predictions about the captivity in Babylon lasting seventy years. Although Daniel is likely uncertain about the exact time schedule, he knows that the captivity has lasted nearly seventy years. He realizes that the promise of God for deliverance must be forthcoming. Now if I had been Daniel, I would have thrown a going-home party. Or I would have made a giant sheet with a prophetic chart and had a prophecy conference in Babylon. I would have shown everyone the predictions of Jeremiah. Daniel does not celebrate, and he does not communicate it to others. When he reads God's Word, he is moved to respond in prayer.

Prayer is my response to God's Word. Eugene Peterson, in a book on pastoral ministry, describes prayer this way: "Prayer is never the first word. It is always the second word. God has the first word. Prayer is 'answering speech.' It is not primarily 'address,' it is 'response.'"

Prayer does not begin with me jumping in and talking to God. Prayer begins with what God has already said in his Word. It becomes my response to God. Think for just a moment about how each of us learns to talk. How do we learn to talk? By listening to other people talk. Children learn to talk by imitating others. How do we learn to talk to God? By listening to God as he talks to us and then imitating his speech.

Eugene Peterson has some interesting thoughts on this dimension of prayer. He suggests that the Old Testament is divided into three sections. The first section is the Torah. The Jews believed that everything God wanted to say is in the Torah. The second section is called the Prophets. The Prophets elaborate on the Torah as it is lived out in historical circumstances. The third section is called the Writings. This section includes the responses of God's people as they lived out the Torah in their historical circumstances. Some of the response is in the form of an argument (the Book of Job). Some of the response is reflective (the Wisdom Literature). And some of the response is prayer (Psalms). Peterson goes on to state that the Book of Psalms was the model for Old Testament prayers as well as the model for Jesus and his disciples. He highly recommends praying through the Psalms as well as other portions of Scripture. Prayer is listening to God in his Word and then responding.

Prayer Is Giving My Undivided Attention to God

"So I turned to the Lord God" (Dan. 9:3). This phrase could also be translated, "I turned my *face* to the Lord God." Prayer is turning my face toward God and in so doing, turning away from everyone and everything else. It is giving God my undivided attention. Prayer is a bit like golf. In golf, you have to put all distractions out of your mind and keep your eye on the ball. The same is true with prayer. You must put all distractions out of your mind and keep your eye on God.

Prayer Is Demonstrating Humility before God

The text states that Daniel turned his face to God "in fasting, and in sackcloth and ashes" (Dan. 9:3).

    fasting—going without food
    sackcloth—wearing coarse, uncomfortable, rough garments
    ashes—putting the ashes of burnt wood on your head

Going without food and wearing sackcloth and ashes was an important way of showing humility before God. In our culture, we do not wear sackcloth and ashes, but fasting is still a relevant prayer principle. We live in an age of gluttony and indulgence. We live in an age of personal convenience. Well, prayer is *not* always convenient, and sometimes it demands fasting. The Bible gives several important reasons for fasting:

1. It helps us focus on God.

Speak unto all the people of the land, and to the priests, saying, When ye fasted and mourned in the fifth and seventh month, even those seventy years, did ye at all fast unto me, even to me?

Zechariah 7:5 KJV

2. It promotes humility.

When I weep and fast,
  I must endure scorn.
    Psalm 69:10

3. It increases our faith.

And he said unto them, "This kind can come forth by nothing, but by prayer and fasting."

Mark 9:29 KJV

Prayer Is Recognizing the Greatness of God

I prayed to the LORD my God and confessed:

"O Lord, the great and awesome God, who keeps his covenant of love with all who love him and obey his commands. . . ."

Daniel 9:4

Prayer begins with the recognition that God is a great God. Note the word *awesome* in the text. He is a great and awesome God! But more than that, he is also a good God. He is faithful to those who love him and to those who keep his commandments. It is one thing to have a great God, but it's something else to have a great God who is good to us. A great God who is interested and concerned about our lives. A great and awesome God who faithfully keeps his covenant, extends his love, fulfills his promise, and is vitally involved and interested in our lives. This is precisely what is said in Hebrews:

And without faith it is impossible to please God, because anyone who comes to him must believe that he exists and that he rewards those who earnestly seek him.

Hebrews 11:6

He is a great God. He exists. But he is also a good God—he rewards and he moves in our lives in response to prayer. He rewards those who earnestly seek him. What is prayer? It is my response to God's Word; it is turning my attention to God; it is coming in humility and brokenness; and it is recognizing that God is great and good.

So you have three options when you come to God, and those options are on a continuum. There are those who say, "The whole idea that God exists is far-fetched. I seriously question his existence. I'm not sure that prayer does a whole lot of good anyway. I tried it once or twice and nothing happened." I talked to someone recently who said, "I prayed. God never answered my prayers. He probably doesn't exist." In this case there is a complete lack of faith. God doesn't exist. If he does, prayer doesn't do any good. I meet people at the other end of the continuum who have complete faith and no doubt. In fact, I envy them. When it comes to prayer, and when it comes to faith, they believe and never doubt. There are a few people who have total faith and no doubt.

But most of the Christians I meet, myself included, are somewhere in the middle. We are not down at the one end where we doubt his existence or doubt prayer. Nor are we at the other end where we have absolute, complete faith with no doubt. I find that my life is lived in the tension in between. There are times of great faith and little doubt. There are times of darkness, of discouragement, of silence, of questions, of misunderstanding, and of not knowing what God is doing. I find myself praying with faith and a lot of questions. I have doubts.

What does God say? "Sorry Ed, it's 100 percent or nothing." You know what Jesus said? "It's not the size of your faith that counts. If you have faith like a little tiny mustard seed, you can remove high mountains." It's not the size of my faith that counts. It's the location of my faith that counts. There was such a man who came to Jesus, and Jesus said, "Do you believe that I can heal you?" It was a gutsy answer. He said, "Yes, I do, but please help my unbelief and doubt." What did Jesus do? Did he say, "Hey, sorry, buddy, it's all or nothing." No! Jesus healed him. We can bring our struggles, our questions, and our doubts to him. He is a great God, and he is a good God.

Prayer begins by recognizing the greatness of God. Note the three names used to address God in this prayer (see Dan. 9:4). They reveal much about this great God.

1. *LORD*—A capital *L*, a capital *O*, a capital *R*, and a capital *D*. It is the translation of the Hebrew word *Jehovah*, which speaks of God's eternal faithfulness to his people. It speaks of the promise of God. Jehovah is the self-existent eternal God who is faithful to his Word. He will not let you down. Every time you see the word in the Bible, capital *L*, capital *O*, capital *R*, capital *D*, it is the word *Jehovah*, and it reminds you of his *promise*.
2. *God*—It's the word *El*. It is the name to which the word *awesome* is attached. The word *God* refers to the fact that God is mighty and powerful. So whenever you find the word *God* in Scripture, the focus is on the power, might, and strength of the one who rules the universe. The key word is *power*.
3. *Lord*—It is capital *L*, small *o*, small *r*, small *d*. It is different from the first name (*LORD*). In the Hebrew language it is the word *Adonai*. It speaks of the fact that God is the ruler of the universe. He is the king. He oversees all of the events of human history. It speaks of God's *program* on the earth. He is in control.

Think about those three words for God: *Jehovah*—his promise; *El*—his power; *Adonai*—his program. The God to whom we pray is the one who keeps his promise. He is the one who is all powerful. He is the one who is involved in the events of human history and in the circumstances of my life. That gives me great encouragement to pray. God is faithful to his word; he doesn't change. God is powerful; there is no problem that he cannot solve. And he is personally interested in my life.

Prayer Is Confession of Sin

We have developed a low view of confession in the twentieth century. We have reduced confession to just saying we're sorry. Let me illustrate from a fictitious family. I'll pick some names at random.

Sally is on level five of a video game. She is really doing well. She has all sorts of bullets and extra lives. Things are going wonderfully. Her five-year-old brother, Fred, walks into the den. As he goes by, he punches reset. Now if you are a parent, you have gone through these experiences. Sally is furious, and she calls for you. So you take Fred aside for your parental lecture:

"Fred, was that a nice thing to do?" you ask.

"Not really," he replies.

"Well, I think you ought to apologize to Sally and tell her you're sorry."

"I'm sorry," Fred mutters, as he walks out of the room.

Is that true repentance? No. Is he really sorry? No. But life goes on. I think we treat confession of sin the same way. We give God a superficial, "I'm sorry," and walk out of the prayer room, and life goes on. Notice, however, the depth of Daniel's confession. You will be tempted to skip over it and get to the analysis. Don't do it. Read it carefully.

> We have sinned and done wrong. We have been wicked and have rebelled; we have turned away from your commands and laws. We have not listened to your servants the prophets, who spoke in your name to our kings, our princes and our fathers, and to all the people of the land.
>
> Lord, you are righteous, but this day we are covered with shame—the men of Judah and people of Jerusalem and all Israel, both near and far, in all the countries where you have scattered us because of our unfaithfulness to you. O Lord, we and our kings, our princes and our fathers are covered with shame because we have sinned against you. The Lord our God is merciful and forgiving, even though we have rebelled against him; we have not obeyed the Lord our God or kept the laws he gave us through his servants the prophets. All Israel has transgressed your law and turned away, refusing to obey you.
>
> Therefore the curses and sworn judgments written in the Law of Moses, the servant of God, have been poured out on us, because we have sinned against you. You have fulfilled the words spoken against us and against our rulers by bringing upon us great disaster. Under the whole heaven nothing has ever been done like what has been done to Jerusalem. Just as it is written in the Law of Moses, all this disaster has come upon us, yet we have not sought the favor of the Lord our God by turning from our sins and giving attention to your truth. The Lord did not hesitate to bring the disaster upon us, for the Lord our God is righteous in everything he does; yet we have not obeyed him.
>
> Daniel 9:5–14

There are four main characteristics of Daniel's confession. These are the elements that should be included in our confession of sin.

1. *We must identify our sin.* Daniel uses four different words to describe sin (v. 5). First of all, he says, "We have sinned." This word means to "miss the mark." Second, he says, "and done wrong." This is more than

missing the mark. It is moving and rearranging the mark. Third, Daniel says, "We have been wicked." This word means passionate rebellion against God. Fourth, Daniel says, "and have rebelled." This word means to reject authority. In fact, he goes on to define this rebellion, "We have turned away from your commands and laws." Daniel says, "We have missed our mark. We have distorted the truth. We have been passionate in our rebellion against you. We have rejected authority. We have ignored and disobeyed your commandments. We have sinned against you." Confession involves an honest identification of sin—by name.

Where did Daniel learn to confess his sin like this? Actually, the first three verbs that he uses to confess sin are found in another prayer recorded earlier in Scripture. Daniel's prayer may have been a repetition of that earlier prayer.

> When they sin against you—for there is no one who does not sin—and you become angry with them and give them over to the enemy, who takes them captive to his own land, far away or near; and if they have a change of heart in the land where they are held captive, and repent and plead with you in the land of their conquerors and say, "We have sinned, we have done wrong, we have acted wickedly. . . ."
>
> 1 Kings 8:46–47

It is reasonable to assume that Daniel had memorized this prayer as a youth. Now he repeats that prayer to God. Prayer can include the repeating and quoting of scriptural prayers.

2. *We must acknowledge our shame.* In verses 7 and 8, the word *shame* occurs twice:

> Lord, you are righteous, but this day we are covered with shame—the men of Judah and people of Jerusalem and all Israel, both near and far, in all the countries where you have scattered us because of our unfaithfulness to you. O LORD, we and our kings, our princes and our fathers are covered with shame because we have sinned against you.
>
> Daniel 9:7–8

The King James Version translates the concept of shame by saying, "confusion of faces." Do you remember when you were in school and had classes where you did not have an earthly idea what the teacher was talking about? She was up there lecturing—all enthusiastic about her subject. But for you it was absolutely irrelevant. You had no idea what she was talking about. You were afraid that she was going to call on you to solve a problem or to respond to a question. So what did you do? I know what I did. I opened my notebook, got my pen out, put my head down, and wrote like mad anything that came to my mind. It had nothing to do with what she was saying up front. I wanted to imply that I was so into the lecture, so deeply moved by this earthshaking information that I couldn't take notes quickly enough—to cover up my confusion of face. It was keeping my head down to hide my face. This is precisely the meaning of *shame*. It is keeping your head down to hide your face before God.

This "confusion of face" comes when we ponder the righteousness of God. "Lord, you are righteous, but this day we are covered with shame" (Dan. 9:7). I must see my life before God—not others. You see, if you compare your life to Ed Dobson, chances are you will not feel a whole lot of shame. I think we have a tendency to compare ourselves with others. "Well, I'm not quite as bad as that person." We don't bow our heads. We are not covered with shame, because on the continuum of human behavior, we are not real bad. However, once I identify my sin, the second part of confession is to place my life before the absolute righteousness and holiness of God.

When I begin to understand that my sin is missing God's standard and it is an offense to God, then I begin to sense the shame of what I have done. It is only when I stand before God that I can say with the prophet Isaiah, "Woe is me!" (Isa. 6:5 KJV). Not the person next to me. It is *me*. When I stand before God's righteousness, and when I think of my sin, my doing wrong, my wickedness, my rebellion, and when I think of the way I have turned from God's Word and have rejected his prophets, I am embarrassed. I am covered with shame. My face is in confusion because I stand before God's holiness and righteousness. That's more than saying, "Yeah, I messed up, I'm sorry. Okay—get over it." It is saying, "O God, I have offended you, and I am covered with shame."

3. *We must appeal to God's mercy.*

The Lord our God is merciful and forgiving, even though we have rebelled against him; we have not obeyed the LORD our God or kept the laws he gave us through his servants the prophets.

Daniel 9:9–10

Again, I like the King James Version of these verses. The words *merciful* and *forgiving* are plural. "To the Lord our God belong mercies and forgivenesses" (v. 9). God's mercies and God's forgivenesses are like the ocean. It is wave after wave after wave of mercy and forgiveness. What an exciting thought! God's mercies are new every day. God's forgiveness is available at any moment. God does not say, "I have one act of mercy, and I have one act of forgiveness. You use it up, no refund, it's over with!" We would be in a mess if God dealt with us that way—if, when we came to God with our sin, our shame, our brokenness, and our repentance, and we cried out to the mercies of God and God said, "The last time you came you used up all the mercy I had. The last time you came you used up all the forgiveness available." Confession is recognizing that the mercies and the forgiveness of God come in wave after wave. Whatever you have done, whatever the condition of your relationship to God, whatever the problems you bring to him, his mercy is broader than your sin. His forgiveness is greater than your sin.

4. *We must affirm God's judgment (justice)*. Note the italicized words in the text.

> All Israel has transgressed your law and turned away, refusing to obey you.
>
> Therefore the curses and sworn judgments written in the Law of Moses, the servant of God, have been poured out on us, because we have sinned against you. You have fulfilled the words spoken against us and against our rulers by bringing upon us great disaster. Under the whole heaven nothing has ever been done like what has been done to Jerusalem. Just as it is written in the Law of Moses, all this disaster has come upon us, yet we have not sought the favor of the LORD our God by turning from our sins and giving attention to your truth. The LORD did not hesitate to bring the disaster upon us, for the LORD our God *is righteous in everything he does;* yet we have not obeyed him.
>
> Daniel 9:11–14, italics added

God brought curses, judgment, and anger against his people. Yet the text says that "the LORD our God is righteous in everything he does." God is just, and part of his justice includes his judgment. Daniel is quoting from the Scripture in making these statements.

If you fully obey the LORD your God and carefully follow all his commands I give you today, the LORD your God will set you high above all the nations on earth. All these blessings will come upon you and accompany you if you obey the LORD your God:

> You will be blessed in the city and blessed in the country.
> The fruit of your womb will be blessed, and the crops of your land and the young of your livestock—the calves of your herds and the lambs of your flocks.
> Your basket and your kneading trough will be blessed.
> You will be blessed when you come in and blessed when you go out.

> Deuteronomy 28:1–6

Living by God's principles brings blessing. Would you agree with that? If I live my life by the principles of God, the result is the blessing of God. Righteousness exalts a nation! Living by God's principles in a nation, a family, a business, and our personal lives brings God's blessing. We like that. We do not like the converse.

However, if you do not obey the LORD your God and do not carefully follow all his commands and decrees I am giving you today, all these curses will come upon you and overtake you:

> You will be cursed in the city and cursed in the country.
> Your basket and your kneading trough will be cursed.
> The fruit of your womb will be cursed, and the crops of your land, and the calves of your herds and the lambs of your flocks.
> You will be cursed when you come in and cursed when you go out.

> Deuteronomy 28:15–19

Disobeying God's principles brings judgment. Now you cannot have one without the other. We tend to focus on a dimension of theology that some people term prosperity theology. We focus exclusively on the fact that if I obey God's principles, if I live by God's Word, then I receive God's blessing. But the opposite is true as well. If I choose to sin, if I choose to disobey, if I choose to distort the truth, if I reject authority, if

I choose to live my life as a believer apart from God's Word, then it will bring God's judgment! God is absolutely righteous in what he does.

We have a pretty difficult time with this principle of judgment. We tend to think of God as the great grandfather in the sky. I remember growing up, when I would not do what my dad expected, he disciplined me. Many times. And rightfully so. As I look back, I appreciate what my dad did in correcting me. What I do not appreciate is that he is now a grandfather, and when my kids do some of the wrong things that I did, he thinks they're cute. When I try to intervene and discipline them, he says, "Give the kid a break, he's so cute." It is the grandparent syndrome.

We think of God in those terms. He is a kindly grandfather who says, "Well, Ed, I know you messed up, and I know you've sinned, but don't worry about it. It's not all that bad. After all, we all struggle in life. Just do the best you can and don't worry about it. Nothing is going to happen." Not so with God. He is faithful to his Word, and his Word says,

> Do not be deceived: God cannot be mocked. A man reaps what he sows. The one who sows to please his sinful nature, from that nature will reap destruction; the one who sows to please the Spirit, from the Spirit will reap eternal life.
>
> Galatians 6:7–8

There is a dimension to the character of God that includes his justice, his judgment, his anger, and his righteousness. When I disobey his commandments, I come under the consequences of that disobedience, which is his judgment.

For us anger is impulsive, arbitrary, and vengeful. Therefore, we assume that God's anger must be impulsive, arbitrary, or vengeful. Not at all! Suppose the Michigan State Police and the Highway Department decided that they were going to do away with all speed limit signs. They would take all the signs down. You would just have to guess how fast to go. One day, you get pulled over by the state police for going sixty-five miles an hour. The policeman announces you were going ten miles over the speed limit. "Well, how was I supposed to know that? There are no signs," you say. "Doesn't make any difference. We decided through here it's fifty-five miles an hour," he says. You would hire the best attorney in town. This is absolutely unfair. There is no warning. There are no signs.

God has placed the speed limit signs all along the highway of life. They are in his Word. When I disobey the principles of God's Word, I deserve the consequences of that disobedience. God is not arbitrary. He is not impulsive. He has not left us in the dark. He has placed his Word all along the highway, and when I disobey, God is righteous. He is just, and I will suffer the consequences.

If sin is not all that serious, and if the consequences do not really matter, and if the judgment of God is not all that significant, then the cross is an absolute waste of time. If God is not righteous and sin is not serious and judgment is not real, then the death of Jesus has been in vain. I can only understand the love and warmth of forgiveness against the background of the darkness of my own sin. You know how serious God is about sin? He sent his only Son into the world to die on the cross. Christ shed his blood. He was buried, and he rose again. This was the only way God could redeem me.

Prayer includes the confession of our sin. What is confession?

1. I must identify my sin by name.
2. I must acknowledge my shame.
3. I must appeal to God's mercy.
4. I must affirm God's judgment and justice.

Prayer Is Appealing to the Working of God in Human History

> Now, O Lord our God, who brought your people out of Egypt with a mighty hand and who made for yourself a name that endures to this day, we have sinned, we have done wrong. O Lord, in keeping with all your righteous acts, turn away your anger and your wrath from Jerusalem, your city, your holy hill. Our sins and the iniquities of our fathers have made Jerusalem and your people an object of scorn to all those around us.
>
> Daniel 9:15–16

Daniel's appeal for God to answer his prayer is rooted in the working of God in human history. Daniel says, "Look what you did before, God! You brought your people out of Egypt. You delivered them. Now do it again!"

God is not removed from human history. Whatever circumstance I face, others have found the same circumstances and have found God to be faithful to his Word. Your situation is not isolated from centuries of human history. God has intervened in the past. He has worked on behalf of his people. He is righteous in everything he does. He has delivered people in generation after generation, and he is capable of working in our lives today. Prayer appeals to the working of God in human history. By the way, that's why the Scriptures are so important when it comes to prayer, because they contain the record of the workings of God in human history. As I read what God did for Abraham, Isaac, Jacob, Moses, Miriam, David, Solomon, Daniel, Mary, and the apostles, I am encouraged that he will meet my need as well.

When you bring your struggles to God in prayer, meditate on what God has done in the past. Psalm 77 is a good passage to read and study in this regard.

> I cried out to God for help;
>   I cried out to God to hear me.
> When I was in distress, I sought the
>   Lord;
>   at night I stretched out untiring
>   hands
>   and my soul refused to be
>   comforted.
>   verse 1

Notice the problem in verses 7 and 8. He feels isolated. God does not appear to be listening.

> Will the Lord reject forever?
>   Will he never show his favor
>   again?
> Has his unfailing love vanished
>   forever?
> Has his promise failed for all time?

The psalmist says, "I cried to the Lord in my distress. I was hurting, but heaven was silent. There was no answer." So what do we do when in our distress we call to God? It is as if our prayers hit the ceiling. It is as if God has failed in his love. There is no response. What do we do? Look at verse 12.

I will meditate on all your works
  and consider all your mighty
    deeds.

I will think about your working in human history.

Your ways, O God, are holy.
  What god is so great as our God?
You are the God who performs
    miracles;
  you display your power among
    the peoples.
                    verses 13–14

You led your people like a flock
  by the hand of Moses and Aaron.
                    verse 20

You know what David says? When I am in distress, when I call and
there is no answer, I will meditate, I will ponder your works, I will think
of your power, your miracles, and your workings in human history. We
do that by reading the Scriptures—the stories of how God has always
been faithful to his people. Daniel confesses his sin, and he says, "Now
God, you have always been righteous in what you did. You have always
intervened. You have always delivered your people. I'm not asking you
to do something unusual or radically different. I am simply asking you
to do for me and for Israel what you have been in the habit of doing all
along." Prayer is appealing to the working of God in human history.

Prayer Is Accepting the Reasons God Answers Us

I must accept the reasons that God answers prayer. Why does God
answer prayer? Someone will say, "He answers prayer if we bug him
long enough. If we pray long enough. If we go after him long enough,
he finally caves in and answers prayer." Someone else might say, "God
just likes to give us stuff. He is like a candy machine. He has unlimited
resources. We come to God in prayer, and the reason God answers prayer
is for our benefit. He helps us climb the mountain. He helps us cross the
river." God answers prayer for the benefit of his people.

According to Daniel, neither of these is the real reason why God answers prayer. Now, prayer does benefit us. But that is a secondary reason that God answers. In fact, Daniel gives three significant reasons why God answers prayer, and none of the reasons have to do with the benefit of Ed Dobson.

1. *God answers prayer for his own glory.*

> Now, our God, hear the prayers and petitions of your servant. For your sake, O Lord, look with favor on your desolate sanctuary.
>
> Daniel 9:17

"For your sake." This is one reason God answers prayer. For his own sake. God is glorified when he responds to the prayers of his people. The prophet Isaiah states the same thing in his writings:

> For my own sake, for my own sake,
>   I do this.
> How can I let myself be defamed?
> I will not yield my glory to
>   another.
>
> Isaiah 48:11

2. *God answers prayer because of his mercies.*

> Give ear, O God, and hear; open your eyes and see the desolation of the city that bears your Name. We do not make requests of you because we are righteous, but because of your great mercy.
>
> Daniel 9:18

Daniel says, "Lord we need you to intervene in our lives. Not because we deserve it. But please answer our prayer because you are a God of mercy." There is no focus on what I deserve. No focus on my rights. No focus on "God owes me something." Prayer is for the glory of God. God answers, not because I deserve it—because I don't. God answers prayer because he is God. Out of the resources of his mercy, he is pleased for his sake and for his glory to answer prayer.

3. *God answers prayer for his reputation.*

> O Lord, listen! O Lord, forgive! O Lord, hear and act! For your sake, O my God, do not delay, because your city and your people bear your Name.
>
> Daniel 9:19

You know what Daniel is saying? "God, you made a lot of promises to Abraham, to Isaac, to Jacob, to Joseph. You made a lot of promises to David. You made promises through Jeremiah that you would be faithful to your people. God, if you forsake us, if you ignore us, if you leave us in bondage, if you do not fulfill your word, all of the pagan nations will laugh. God, I am asking you to answer prayer, number one, for your glory, number two, for your mercy, and, number three, because we bear your name and your reputation is at stake. For your reputation, O God, intervene and answer prayer."

Moses also appealed to God's reputation in prayer. After the Israelites had made a golden calf and worshiped it, God was angry. He told Moses he was going to start over with just Moses. Note the following request of Moses:

> But Moses sought the favor of the LORD his God. "O LORD," he said, "why should your anger burn against your people, whom you brought out of Egypt with great power and a mighty hand? Why should the Egyptians say, 'It was with evil intent that he brought them out, to kill them in the mountains and to wipe them off the face of the earth'? Turn from your fierce anger; relent and do not bring disaster on your people. Remember your servants Abraham, Isaac and Israel, to whom you swore by your own self: 'I will make your descendants as numerous as the stars in the sky and I will give your descendants all this land I promised them, and it will be their inheritance forever.'" Then the LORD relented and did not bring on his people the disaster he had threatened.
>
> Exodus 32:11–14

Prayer Is Leaving My Request with God

> While I was speaking and praying, confessing my sin and the sin of my people Israel and making my request to the LORD my God for his holy hill. . . .
>
> Daniel 9:20

The phrase "making my request to the LORD" could also be translated, "laying down my request before the Lord." It is releasing my requests to God. I heard a Pentecostal preacher many years ago give some good advice on prayer. He said this:

When you are praying, get out a legal pad or a piece of paper. Write out your requests in sentence or paragraph form. Write them out to the Lord. Whatever the struggle is. Whatever the problem is. Whatever you are facing. Write out what you are asking God to do. Then take that page or pages and put it in your hand. Lift your hands up to the Lord. This is symbolic of the fact that you are taking all of your requests and all of your needs and all of your heartaches and all of your problems and laying them down before the Lord.

Let go and let God.

Prayer Gets Results

While I was still in prayer, Gabriel, the man I had seen in the earlier vision, came to me in swift flight about the time of the evening sacrifice. He instructed me and said to me, "Daniel, I have now come to give you insight and understanding. As soon as you began to pray, an answer was given, which I have come to tell you, for you are highly esteemed. Therefore, consider the message and understand the vision."

Daniel 9:21–23

God now answers Daniel's prayer by giving him wisdom and insight. When I pray to God, he either intervenes in my life, or he gives me insight. One or the other, or both. When I pray and God does not intervene, perhaps he is communicating to me another answer. He wants me to have insight in one of these areas.

Insight into God's Word

Sometimes his answer of nonintervention is for the purpose of giving me new insight into his Word. That's what happened to Daniel. He is reading Jeremiah. He prays to God and claims the promise. God then gives him a vision far larger than what he had read in the writing of Jeremiah. It is new insight into God's Word.

In the struggles of our lives when God does not intervene, and we pray and believe and trust him, and the healing does not come, God may want us to go back into his Word and discover new insights. If you have walked with the Lord very long, you know what I am talking about. You can read a passage of Scripture over and over. You can parse the verbs. You can exegete the passage. You can quote the theology. You have even memorized it. All of a sudden you face a crisis in your life and you come back to that passage, and it is as if a light bulb goes on in your mind. You see new insight. You see new wisdom. You see new principles. You see new ideas in God's Word.

Insight into Who God Is

Sometimes when God does not intervene as we want him to, he answers our prayer with new insight into who he is. His character. His being. There are dimensions of God's character that are revealed through prayer. When God works the miracle we need, we become aware of his power. When God does not work the miracle we need, we become aware of his strength to see us through the difficulty.

Insight into Who We Are

Sometimes when God does not intervene, he wants us to get insight into who *we* are. When everything is going our way, we tend not to examine ourselves. We tend to take everything for granted. When God knocks the props out of our lives and he does not intervene to immediately rebuild them as we want him to, sometimes it is for the purpose of giving us insight into who we are. Areas of our lives that are displeasing to him. Sins that are unconfessed. Decisions that need to be made. Priorities that need to be changed. When we go through that struggle, we come out the other side with wisdom and insight into who we are. God always answers, but sometimes it is insight, not intervention.

Paul provides a wonderful case study of unanswered prayer. He has a problem. He doesn't like the problem. He prays about the problem. God does not intervene. But God does answer his prayer with insight into his Word, into his character, and into Paul himself.

> To keep me from becoming conceited because of these surpassingly great revelations, there was given me a thorn in my flesh, a messenger of Satan, to torment me. Three times I pleaded with the Lord to take it away from me.
> 2 Corinthians 12:7–8

Paul has a problem. He prays three times.

> But he said to me, . . .
> verse 9

Paul is about to receive insight into God's Word. "I am not going to heal you, I am not going to do away with it, but I am going to answer your prayer. Number one, I am going to give you insight into my Word. What is that insight?"

> My grace is sufficient for you, . . .
>   verse 9

"I am, number two, going to give you insight into my character."

> . . . for my power is made perfect in weakness.
>   verse 9

God said to Paul, "I want you to have new insight into my Word, and here it is. You have a problem—my grace is sufficient. That's the principle. I'm going to give you insight into who I am—my power is made perfect in your weakness.
"Number three, I am going to give you insight into yourself."

> Therefore, I will boast all the more gladly about my weaknesses, so that Christ's power may rest on me.
>   verse 9

Notice the insight into himself in verse 10.

> That is why, for Christ's sake, I delight in weaknesses, in insults, in hardships, in persecutions, in difficulties. *For when I am weak, then I am strong.*
>   italics added

Paul says, "Remove it." God says, "No, but I will answer your prayer. I'll give you insight into my Word—my grace is sufficient. I will give you insight into my character—my power is made perfect in your weakness. And I will give you insight into your personal life, and you will discover that it is when you are the weakest that you are the strongest."

Insight

As the Nike commercial says, "Just Do It." Take these principles and include them in your prayer.

1. Prayer is my response to God's Word.
2. Prayer is giving my undivided attention to God.
3. Prayer is demonstrating humility before God.
4. Prayer is recognizing the greatness of God.
5. Prayer is confession of sin.
6. Prayer is appealing to the working of God in human history.
7. Prayer is accepting the reasons God answers us.
8. Prayer is leaving my request with God.
9. Prayer gets results.

Prayer

Lord, teach me to pray like Daniel. Amen.

Part 2

The Prophetic Section of the Book of Daniel

Introduction

Every Thanksgiving Day we eat together as a family. Several years ago my mom and dad had joined us. After we had finished eating, at about two o'clock in the afternoon, I said to my dad, "Would you like to go play golf? It's a beautiful day." He said, "You know, I've always wanted to play golf. I have never played golf in my life, so I would love to go." I got him a pair of sneakers and gave him my son's set of clubs to use.

It was a wonderful time. We were about halfway through when I noticed the person who runs the course coming toward us in a cart. He had someone with him in his cart. I thought, *What in the world have we done? We're going to be thrown off the golf course.* They pulled up, and the guy who runs the course said, "This is so-and-so from the *Grand Rapids Press*. He is doing an article on what people do on Thanksgiving Day. Could he take your photograph?" The next day the front page of the newspaper had a beautiful picture of my dad with his Irish cap, putting on the seventeenth green. The first time he played golf!—front page of the *Grand Rapids Press*!

I will never forget the first hole we played. I put the ball down, got a three wood, whacked the ball, and it went to the far side of the next fairway over. My dad got up and adjusted his cap. I told him how to hold the club. He took a look at the ball, took a swing, and hit the top of the ball. It rolled three or four feet. I said, "Dad, don't worry about it. It's a tough sport. Take another ball and try again." So he set a second ball. Adjusted his cap. Took a swing and missed the ball completely! He looked up at me and with that twinkle in his eye said, "This is a really difficult course."

That's how I feel about the prophetic section of the Book of Daniel. It is a pretty tough course! It is a lot like golf. There are lots of hazards, sand traps, woods, narrow fairways, and difficult greens. But I'm going to take a swing, and I hope I am reasonably on target.

When we think of future events, there are basically three viewpoints. All of them are centered around the word *millennium*. It refers to a period of peace and harmony upon the earth.

The first viewpoint about future events is called the premillennial position. It is as follows: As we look toward the future, Jesus Christ is coming. When he comes, he will establish a kingdom, and his coming will be at the beginning of this millennial period of time. Christ comes *pre* or before the millennium. Many who hold this position (myself included), believe that the next major event will be the rapture of the church. This will be followed by seven years of tribulation. At the end of the seven years, Christ will return to establish his millennial kingdom on the earth. I confess that this is my bias, and it forms the basis for my interpretation of these prophetic chapters.

The second viewpoint in regard to future events is the postmillennial position. This position states that the church will usher in an age of joy and peace upon the earth. Things will get better and better. The church will have greater influence until the kingdoms of this world are brought in some way under the authority of Christ. There will be a lengthy period of joy because of the influence of the church. This is the millennial age. At the end of the age, Jesus will return.

The third viewpoint in regard to future events is the amillennial position. Simply stated—there is no millennium. Jesus will not come back to the earth to establish a kingdom. He will not rule upon the earth. Rather, one day Christ comes, not to establish a kingdom or rule upon the earth, but to begin eternity. There is no kingdom upon the earth.

Whatever your position on future events, I have tried to draw practical insights from these chapters. I approach them from a premillennial point of view. However, there is much we can learn—whatever our perspective.

Chapter Eleven

The Last Days

Daniel 7:1–28

Bible prophecy is a complicated subject. There is a tendency to go to one extreme or the other. There are some who overemphasize the prophecies of Scripture. When they get to a book like Daniel and a chapter like chapter 7, they go into great detail to identify these prophecies. They examine the symbols; they analyze the events; they apply the prophecy to their particular moment in history. In other words, they conclude that what is recorded in Daniel is what is happening right now, and we are living in the last days. This approach has been practiced for almost two thousand years, and so far everyone has been wrong. So I want to be very careful in my interpretation of the prophecies.

The other extreme is to ignore prophecy altogether. Prophecy is complicated. It is difficult to understand. It is hard to interpret. Therefore, let's not worry about it. However, the Bible does contain prophecy, and we must respond to these sections even if they are difficult to understand.

Just the Facts

In the first year of Belshazzar king of Babylon, Daniel had a dream, and visions passed through his mind as he was lying on his bed. He wrote down the substance of his dream.

Daniel said: "In my vision at night I looked, and there before me were the four winds of heaven churning up the great sea. Four great beasts, each different from the others, came up out of the sea."

Daniel 7:1–3

Daniel's dream centers around three symbols: the wind, the sea, and four beasts.

1. *The wind.* Throughout the Bible, wind is symbolic of the power and sovereignty of God. It often represents God's working in the events of human history.

But God remembered Noah and all the wild animals and the livestock that were with him in the ark, and he sent a wind over the earth, and the waters receded.

Genesis 8:1

God protected Noah, his family, and the animals from the flood. The rest of the world is destroyed. Then God causes a wind to blow so that the waters of the flood will recede. This wind represents the movement of God after the flood.

So Moses stretched out his staff over Egypt, and the LORD made an east wind blow across the land all that day and all that night. By morning the wind had brought the locusts.

Exodus 10:13

Moses then left Pharaoh and prayed to the LORD. And the LORD changed the wind to a very strong west wind, which caught up the locusts and carried them into the Red Sea. Not a locust was left anywhere in Egypt.

Exodus 10:18–19

God uses the wind to accomplish his purpose. It is a tangible demonstration of his power and sovereignty in the events of people and nations.

2. *The sea.* The second symbol in this dream is the sea. In the Bible, the sea often represents humanity.

Oh, the raging of many nations—
    they rage like the raging sea!
Oh, the uproar of the peoples—

they roar like the roaring of great
    waters!
Although the peoples roar like the
    roar of surging waters,
  when he rebukes them they flee
    far away,
driven before the wind like chaff on
    the hills,
  like tumbleweed before a gale.
              Isaiah 17:12–13

Notice that both symbols are used in these verses. The nations are represented by the sea, and God's activity is represented by the wind.

3. *The four beasts*. These beasts represent the rise of four different world empires. We will examine them in a moment. When you put all these symbols together, you get a preliminary understanding of Daniel's dream. God moves (the wind) in the events of humanity (the sea) to give rise to four separate kingdoms (four beasts).

L B L B—*Lion, Bear, Leopard, Beast*

The four beasts, which represent four kingdoms, are identified.
1. *The lion* (the Babylonian Empire):

The first was like a lion, and it had the wings of an eagle. I watched until its wings were torn off and it was lifted from the ground so that it stood on two feet like a man, and the heart of a man was given to it.
              Daniel 7:4

2. *The bear* (the Medo-Persian Empire):

And there before me was a second beast, which looked like a bear. It was raised up on one of its sides, and it had three ribs in its mouth between its teeth. It was told, "Get up and eat your fill of flesh!"
              Daniel 7:5

3. *The leopard* (the Greek Empire):

After that, I looked, and there before me was another beast, one that looked like a leopard. And on its back it had four wings like those of a bird. This beast had four heads, and it was given authority to rule.
              Daniel 7:6

4. *The unnamed beast* (the Roman Empire):

After that, in my vision at night I looked, and there before me was a fourth beast—terrifying and frightening and very powerful. It had large iron teeth; it crushed and devoured its victims and trampled underfoot whatever was left. It was different from all the former beasts, and it had ten horns.

Daniel 7:7–8

The descriptions of these kingdoms are similar to the description of Nebuchadnezzar's dream in Daniel chapter 3. In both these overviews of human history, the greatest attention is given to the last empire—the Roman Empire.

What Does God Have to Do with It?

Before Daniel is given understanding in regard to these animals, he is first given a reminder that God is in control. This reminder includes the authority of God, the judgment of God, and the kingdom of God.

The Authority of God

As I looked,
thrones were set in place,
    and the Ancient of Days took his
        seat.
His clothing was as white as snow;
    the hair of his head was white like
        wool.
His throne was flaming with
        fire,
    and its wheels were all
        ablaze.
A river of fire was flowing,
    coming out from before him.
Thousands upon thousands
        attended him;
    ten thousand times ten thousand
        stood before him.
The court was seated,
    and the books were opened.

Daniel 7:9–10

God is described as sitting on a throne. He is in control. He is called the Ancient of Days, which speaks of his eternalness. His clothing and hair are white, speaking of his purity. The multitudes are gathered before him, and he opens the books to judge them.

The Judgment of God

> Then I continued to watch because of the boastful words the horn was speaking. I kept looking until the beast was slain and its body destroyed and thrown into the blazing fire. (The other beasts had been stripped of their authority, but were allowed to live for a period of time.)
>
> Daniel 7:11–12

The beasts that represent the earthly kingdoms are "stripped of their authority." This speaks of the authority of God over earthly kingdoms and his personal involvement in their downfall. God is active in the affairs of nations.

The Kingdom of God

> In my vision at night I looked, and there before me was one like a son of man, coming with the clouds of heaven. He approached the Ancient of Days and was led into his presence. He was given authority, glory and sovereign power; all peoples, nations and men of every language worshiped him. His dominion is an everlasting dominion that will not pass away, and his kingdom is one that will never be destroyed.
>
> Daniel 7:13–14

This is the first time the phrase "son of man" is used. It is a clear reference to the coming of Messiah to establish an everlasting kingdom on the earth. These verses became the hope of the Jewish people that a golden age would be ushered upon the earth by Messiah. Christ takes up this phrase in the New Testament and calls himself the Son of Man (see John 12:23).

The underlying principle of this vision of God is that God is involved in the events of human history and all these events ultimately lead to the coming of Christ. Until he comes, it is not over. From our vantage point we are living in the confusion and turmoil of human history. Kingdoms rise and fall. Earthly dictators come and go. We find ourselves caught in the tension of Middle Eastern conflict and the prospect for peace. At times it looks dark, and at times it looks hopeful. We find ourselves in the tension of human history asking the question, "Is there hope for tomorrow?" The point of this vision is that there is hope for tomorrow! It is not over until the Son of Man comes and until all the kingdoms of this world are delivered to Christ. Until Jesus himself sets up his kingdom and rules forever and ever and ever. It is not over until the King comes.

I am a Notre Dame football fan. Several years ago, Notre Dame was playing Penn State. It was on a Saturday afternoon, but I was disappointed because the finest football team in the nation was playing on television, and I could not see it. I was at the church preparing for our Saturday night service. Someone came and said, "I just heard that Notre Dame is winning big." At that point they were two touchdowns ahead.

We have a couple of Penn State fans in the church. One of them is an attorney who was at home watching the game. I gave her a call because I knew how depressed she would be, given the fact that Notre Dame was absolutely killing Penn State—two touchdowns ahead. She had her answering machine on. So I said, "This is Ed Dobson. I thought I'd give you a ring. I know you're watching the football game, and as a pastor I am compelled to rejoice with those who rejoice and mourn with those who mourn. So I am calling to extend my sympathy and my concern for you. The fact of the matter is brother Joe and the Nittany Lions have absolutely no chance of beating Notre Dame."

After the Saturday night service, I got in my truck to drive home. I flipped on the radio. WMAQ news station was on, and the sports came on with this announcement: In the last four seconds, Penn State kicked a field goal to beat number-one-ranked Notre Dame.

I thought, *You idiot, Dobson! It's not over till it's over.* Then I thought, *Now what should I do? Should I demonstrate humility and repentance and call her?* I decided, *No. I am not going to do that.*

Eight o'clock the next morning I got to my office, and hanging on my office door was a package adorned with Penn State balloons. Inside the package was a Nittany Lion stuffed animal and a card stating "With Deepest Sympathy." The handwritten note read: "Ed, my deepest sympathy. A wise pastor once said, 'The Bible says you should cry with those who cry and rejoice with those who rejoice.' My thoughts are with you in these troubled times. May this Nittany Lion remind you of this day."

I put the lion on my shelf. It reminds me that it's not over till it's over. The final whistle has not blown. It's not over yet! God is ultimately in control, and the God who is in control of human history is moving in my individual life and in the events of human history. One day, Jesus Christ will return. It will be worth it all when we see him.

What Is the Bottom Line?

> I, Daniel, was troubled in spirit, and the visions that passed through my mind disturbed me. I approached one of those standing there and asked him the true meaning of all this.
>
> Daniel 7:15–16

Daniel is troubled by this dream and wants to know what all this means. The text states that he is "troubled in spirit." A literal translation would be, "grieved in my spirit and in the midst of my body." The idea is that his spirit sort of rattled around in his body.

Daniel is told that the four beasts represent four kingdoms that will rise on the earth (see Dan. 7:17). At the end of these four kingdoms, "the saints of the Most High will receive the kingdom and will possess it forever" (see Dan. 7:18). Most commentators believe that these four beasts represent the kingdoms of Babylon, Medo-Persia, Greece, and Rome. This is based on the interpretation of Nebuchadnezzar's dream in chapter 2. After these kingdoms rise and fall, God will establish his kingdom on earth. This is the bottom line of Daniel's vision.

The Fourth Kingdom

Great detail is given about the fourth beast—detail that is not easy to understand or interpret.

> Then I wanted to know the true meaning of the fourth beast, which was different from all the others and most terrifying, with its iron teeth and bronze claws—the beast that crushed and devoured its victims and trampled underfoot whatever was left. I also wanted to know about the ten horns on its head and about the other horn that came up, before which three of them fell—the horn that looked more imposing than the others and that had eyes and a mouth that spoke boastfully. As I watched, this horn was waging war against the saints and defeating them, until the

Ancient of Days came and pronounced judgment in favor of the saints of the Most High, and the time came when they possessed the kingdom.

Daniel 7:19–22

This is strange language. Here is an unusual animal that initially seizes power over the entire world. Out of this animal ten horns emerge. Then an eleventh horn comes along, and three of the ten horns give allegiance to the eleventh horn. The eleventh horn opposes the saints and persecutes them. Then the Ancient of Days pronounces judgment in favor of the saints. What does all this mean? Well, the explanation is given to Daniel (7:23–27). This can be best understood in a series of stages.

Stage 1

He gave me this explanation: "The fourth beast is a fourth kingdom that will appear on earth. It will be different from all other kingdoms and will devour the whole earth, trampling it down and crushing it."

Daniel 7:23

This is the opening stage of the Roman Empire. After the Babylonian Empire has collapsed, after the Medo-Persian Empire has collapsed, and after the Greek Empire has collapsed, there will come another world power. This power will expand over the civilized world until it brings the entire world under its control.

Stage 2

The ten horns are ten kings who will come from this kingdom.

Daniel 7:24

There is apparently an initial phase of world domination by the Roman Empire. These ten horns that represent ten kings are likely a second phase of the Roman Empire. The Scriptures do not state whether this second phase occurs immediately after the original dominations of the Roman Empire, or whether there is a parenthesis in between. It simply states that after Rome dominates the world, there will be a second phase. It will be unique and different from the first. In the second phase of world domination there will be a coalition—a political or economic alignment of individual states or countries. There will be ten in number, and they will grow out of the Roman Empire.

Stage 3

> After them another king will arise, different from the earlier ones; he will subdue three kings.
>
> Daniel 7:24

An eleventh horn now emerges. I believe that this refers to the rise of Antichrist. The reason I believe he represents Antichrist is the description about him in the text:

> He will speak against the Most High and oppress his saints and try to change the set times and the laws. The saints will be handed over to him for a time, times and half a time.
>
> Daniel 7:25

Note the characteristics of this eleventh horn.

1. *"He will speak against the Most High."* The underlying idea in this statement is that this person will attempt to elevate himself to the stature of the Most High God. He will not only oppose God, he will also seek to become God. This is precisely what the New Testament predicts about the coming Antichrist.

> Don't let anyone deceive you in any way, for that day will not come until the rebellion occurs and the man of lawlessness is revealed, the man doomed to destruction. He will oppose and will exalt himself over everything that is called God or is worshiped, so that he sets himself up in God's temple, proclaiming himself to be God.
>
> 2 Thessalonians 2:3–4

2. *He will oppress God's saints.* The verb used in this phrase means to "wear out." It means to hassle, persecute, or oppose.

3. *He will "try to change the set times and the laws."* This likely refers to the changing of natural, civil, and moral laws. It is interesting to note that the New Testament calls Antichrist a "man of lawlessness" (2 Thess. 2:3).

4. *"The saints will be handed over to him."* This persecution will last for "a time, times and half a time" (Dan. 7:25). How long will this be? The same phrase is used in Daniel 12:7. The exact amount of time is outlined later in the chapter—namely 1,290 days (see 12:11). This "times"

is three and one-half (actually seven months) years. Many interpreters believe that "time" equals one year. "Times" equals two or more years. Accepting "times" as two years, "time, times and half a time" would be three and one-half years.

Let us review for just a moment. Daniel says, "I want to know more about this last world empire." Here is the scenario: With power, force, and might Rome will conquer the world. Then out of that empire there will emerge a political coalition of ten separate kingdoms. When that occurs, an eleventh king will come along who will forge an alliance with three countries out of which he ultimately will bring about world domination. When he is elevated to world domination, he will do several things:

1. He will proclaim himself to be a god.
2. He will harass the saints.
3. He will attempt to change the laws.
4. The people of Israel will be delivered over to him to be harassed and persecuted for a specific period of time—namely, three and a half years.

If all of this sounds bleak, it is. But the good news is yet to come.

The Coming of God

> But the court will sit, and his power will be taken away and completely destroyed forever. Then the sovereignty, power and greatness of the kingdoms under the whole heaven will be handed over to the saints, the people of the Most High. His kingdom will be an everlasting kingdom, and all rulers will worship and obey him.
>
> Daniel 7:26–27

God comes in judgment to strip the beast of his power and to establish his own kingdom and authority. There are several characteristics of God's coming that merit note.

1. *He will come in judgment.* The text describes it, "the court will sit."
2. *God will come to set up his kingdom.* He will not come after his kingdom has been established. He will come to set up his kingdom.

3. *His coming will be dramatic.* God's coming will be a dramatic intervention in human history.

4. *He will come in victory and triumph.*

Then the sovereignty, power and greatness of the kingdoms under the whole heaven will be handed over to the saints, the people of the Most High. His kingdom will be an everlasting kingdom, and all rulers will worship and obey him.

Daniel 7:27

Insight

1. *If God can be trusted with the affairs of the universe, he can be trusted with the affairs of my life.* Maybe you are saying, "Well, all of this is interesting. The big horn. The little horn. The three horns. The beast. The lion. The leopard. But I got fired last week. My spouse filed for divorce. I discovered my kids are on drugs. All of this stuff is interesting, but what about my life?" Here is one insight. If God can be trusted with the affairs of the universe, and he can, then he can be trusted with the affairs of my life. God can be trusted in the sweep of human history—the rise and fall of political kingdoms. God can be trusted in the events of history, and you can trust him now in the events of your life. There are several dimensions to this insight.

It is a staggering thought. It is staggering to think that the God of the universe, the God of human history, and the God of world empires is actually interested in my life. David expresses this in the Book of Psalms:

When I consider your heavens,
     the work of your fingers,
the moon and the stars,
     which you have set in place,
what is man that you are mindful of
          him,
     the son of man that you care for
          him?

Psalm 8:3–4

It is an encouraging thought. Knowing that God is interested in me is an encouraging thought. David expresses this well in Psalm 139. He identifies at least three factors about God and us that ought to give us encouragement. First, we should be encouraged because God knows us (vv. 1–4). Second, we should be encouraged because God is with us (v. 7). Third, we ought to be encouraged because God made us (vv. 13, 15–16).

It is an empowering thought.

> Then Jesus came to them and said, "All authority in heaven and on earth has been given to me. Therefore go and make disciples of all nations, baptizing them in the name of the Father and of the Son and of the Holy Spirit, and teaching them to obey everything I have commanded you. And surely I am with you always, to the very end of the age."
>
> Matthew 28:18–20

The reality of God's intent and presence in our lives should empower us for ministry and obedience.

2. *If the prophecies of God come true, then you can rely on his promises.* If the prophecies of Scripture come true (and many of them have), then you can trust the promises of Scripture as well.

> Remember the former things, those
>   of long ago;
>   I am God, and there is no other;
>   I am God, and there is none
>   like me.
> I make known the end from the
>   beginning,
>   from ancient times, what is still to
>   come.
> I say: My purpose will stand,
>   and I will do all that I please.
> From the east I summon a bird of
>   prey;
>   from a far-off land, a man to fulfill
>   my purpose.
> What I have said, that will I bring
>   about;
>   what I have planned, that will
>   I do.
>
> Isaiah 46:9–11

Prayer

God, I am overwhelmed that you have an interest in me. Thank you for the encouragement you give me with your presence. Help me to live today and every day with a continued awareness that you are with me. Amen.

Chapter Twelve

The Rise and Fall of Antichrist

Daniel 8:1–27

The vision of Daniel recorded in chapter 8 is related to the vision recorded in chapter 7. The message of Daniel 7 is that earthly kingdoms will rise and fall until God comes to establish his kingdom. Prior to that event, there will be a renewed coalition of the ancient Roman Empire. Out of that coalition Antichrist will come to power. He will oppose God and persecute the saints (Israel) for three and one-half years. Then God will come in judgment to destroy Antichrist and to establish his kingdom. The vision in chapter 8 focuses on two of the world empires already mentioned—Medo-Persia and Greece. It also deals with the prototype of the coming Antichrist.

> In the third year of King Belshazzar's reign, I, Daniel, had a vision, after the one that had already appeared to me. In my vision I saw myself in the citadel of Susa in the province of Elam; in the vision I was beside the Ulai Canal.
>
> Daniel 8:1–2

The city of Susa is two hundred and thirty miles east of Babylon and one hundred and twenty miles north of the Persian Gulf. The city is in the province of Elam, which is a small and relatively insignificant province in the Babylonian Empire. The Ulai Canal is a hand-dug canal

152

that connects two major rivers and goes through the city of Susa. It is nine hundred feet wide. The vision that Daniel receives in this city is shocking:

> I, Daniel, was exhausted and lay ill for several days. Then I got up and went about the king's business. I was appalled by the vision; it was beyond understanding.
>
> Daniel 8:27

Daniel's mind is blown by what he sees. Why? Daniel is an official in the mighty Empire of Babylon. Babylon seems indestructible. Now Daniel receives a vision about how a tiny and insignificant city is going to emerge into a world power. This seems both impossible and extremely unlikely. Yet this is what he sees.

The Vision

Daniel's vision includes two animals: a ram and a goat. They represent the Medo-Persian and Greek Empires.

The Ram

> I looked up, and there before me was a ram with two horns, standing beside the canal, and the horns were long. One of the horns was longer than the other but grew up later. I watched the ram as he charged toward the west and the north and the south. No animal could stand against him, and none could rescue from his power. He did as he pleased and became great.
>
> Daniel 8:3–4

The ram represents the Medo-Persian Empire (see Dan. 8:20). One of the peculiar features of this ram is that one of its horns is long and the other is short. Then the short horn grows until it is longer and more prominent than the other horn. When Daniel receives this vision, Babylon is the capital city of the mighty Babylonian Empire. North of Babylon is the emerging power of Persia (modern-day Iran). Persia represents the long horn. To the east of Babylon and to the southeast of Persia is the tiny kingdom of Media. This is also known as the province of Elam with its capital city, Susa.

Media is represented by the small horn of the ram. But the small horn (Media) grows. Media forms an alliance with Persia, and under the leadership of Cyrus the Great, it conquers the entire ancient world. Cyrus ascends the throne in Susa in 559 B.C., and by 539 B.C. he has defeated Babylon. The short horn (Media) grows stronger than the large horn (Persia) and eventually conquers the world. It is interesting to note that the guardian spirit of the Persian Empire was a ram with pointed horns. When the Persian king stood at the head of the army, he wore a crown in the shape of a ram's head.

The Goat

As I was thinking about this, suddenly a goat with a prominent horn between his eyes came from the west, crossing the whole earth without touching the ground. He came toward the two-horned ram I had seen standing beside the canal and charged at him in great rage. I saw him attack the ram furiously, striking the ram and shattering his two horns. The ram was powerless to stand against him; the goat knocked him to the ground and trampled on him, and none could rescue the ram from his power. The goat became very great, but at the height of his power his large horn was broken off, and in its place four prominent horns grew up toward the four winds of heaven. Out of one of them came another horn, which started small but grew in power to the south and to the east and toward the Beautiful Land.

Daniel 8:5–9

The goat probably represents Alexander the Great. Alexander was twenty when he ascended the throne in Macedonia. His teacher was Aristotle. Aristotle told Alexander the Great that you can rule the world if you get the people of the world to adopt the Greek language and culture. This is precisely what Alexander set out to do. At age twenty, with his armies, he began to conquer the world. Thirteen years later he is in the city of Babylon, and he has conquered the entire ancient world. He does it with lightning speed (see Dan. 8:5). He never loses a single battle. No one can stand in his way.

The city of Tyre is an example of Alexander's power. Nebuchadnezzar besieged this city for thirteen years and never could conquer it. Alexander conquers it in a few months and burns the entire city to the ground. After thirteen years, at age thirty-three, Alexander controls the entire world. But something happens. The text predicts that in the height of his power he will be broken off (see Dan. 8:8). At age thirty-three, he gets a fever. He goes into a drunken stupor, and he dies. This occurs in the city of Babylon. His generals divide the kingdom into four parts (see Dan. 8:8).

The Prototype of Antichrist

> Out of one of them came another horn, which started small but grew in power to the south and to the east and toward the Beautiful Land. It grew until it reached the host of the heavens, and it threw some of the starry host down to the earth and trampled on them. It set itself up to be as great as the Prince of the host; it took away the daily sacrifice from him, and the place of his sanctuary was brought low. Because of rebellion, the host of the saints and the daily sacrifice were given over to it. It prospered in everything it did, and truth was thrown to the ground.
>
> Daniel 8:9–12

Many commentators agree that the horn described in these verses is Antiochus Epiphanes. Antiochus was headquartered in ancient Syria. His brother, Seleucus Philopater, was the king of Syria. Seleucus was murdered. His son, Demetrius, was the rightful heir to the throne, but he was being held hostage in Rome. During this turbulent time, Antiochus seized the throne. He added the word *Epiphanes* to his title. This word means "the illustrious one." In addition to his role in human history, Antiochus is also a prototype of the future Antichrist.

His Rise to Power

> Out of one of them came another horn, which started small but grew in power to the south and to the east and toward the Beautiful Land.
>
> Daniel 8:9

He conquers to the south (Egypt), to the east (Armenia), and to the "Beautiful Land" (Palestine). The ancient historical records of Antiochus Epiphanes describe battles in all these geographic areas.

His Oppression

> It grew until it reached the host of the heavens, and it threw some of the starry host down to the earth and trampled on them.
>
> Daniel 8:10

This is a strange verse. After conquering various territories, Antiochus Epiphanes reaches the "host of the heavens" and throws down some of the stars and tramples them. What does this mean? I believe that the stars of heaven represent the Jewish people.

> Then the word of the LORD came to him: "This man will not be your heir, but a son coming from your own body will be your heir." He took him outside and said, "Look up at the heavens and count the stars—if indeed you can count them." Then he said to him, "So shall your off-spring be."
>
> Genesis 15:4–5

Antiochus opposes the Jewish people and begins to harass and persecute them. The terror of these days is recorded in the Book of Maccabees.

> There were also seven brothers who were arrested with their mother. The king tried to force them to taste pig's flesh, which the Law forbids, by tor-turing them with whips and scourges. One of them, acting as spokesman for the others, said, "What are you trying to find out from us? We are pre-pared to die rather than break the laws of our ancestors." The king, in a fury, ordered pans and cauldrons to be heated over a fire. As soon as they were red-hot he commanded that this spokesman of theirs should have his tongue cut out, his head scalped and his extremities cut off, while the other brothers and his mother looked on. When he had been rendered completely helpless, the king gave orders for him to be brought, still breathing, to the fire and fried alive in a pan. As the smoke from the pan drifted about, his mother and the rest encouraged one another to die nobly, with such words as these, "The Lord God is watching, and surely he takes pity on us, as in the song in which Moses bore witness against the people to their face, pro-claiming that 'he will certainly take pity on his servants.'"
>
> 2 Maccabees 7:1–6 JB

His Desolation

> It set itself up to be as great as the Prince of the host; it took away the daily sacrifice from him, and the place of his sanctuary was brought low. Because of rebellion, the host of the saints and the daily sacrifice were given over to it. It prospered in everything it did, and truth was thrown to the ground.
>
> Daniel 8:11–12

He set himself up to be "as great as the Prince of the host" (v. 11). This means he elevated himself to the stature of a god. He had coins distributed for circulation that had the inscription "Theos Antiochus, Theos Epiphanes," which means "Antiochus—God manifest (revealed)." He took away the sacrifice from the temple and desecrated the altar by offering pigs for sacrifices. The Book of Maccabees describes these dark days.

> Then the king issued a proclamation to his whole kingdom that all were to become a single people, each renouncing his particular customs. All the pagans conformed to the king's decree, and many Israelites chose to accept his religion, sacrificing to idols and profaning the sabbath. The king also sent instructions by messenger to Jerusalem and the towns of Judah directing them to adopt customs foreign to the country, banning holocausts, sacrifices and libations from the sanctuary, profaning sabbaths and feasts, defiling the sanctuary and the sacred ministers, building altars, precincts and shrines for idols, sacrificing pigs and unclean beasts, leaving their sons uncircumcised, and prostituting themselves to all kinds of impurity and abomination, so that they should forget the Law and revoke all observance of it. Anyone not obeying the king's command was to be put to death. Writing in such terms to every part of his kingdom, the king appointed inspectors for the whole people, and directed all the towns of Judah to offer sacrifice one after another.
>
> 1 Maccabees 1:41–54 JB

His Defeat

> Then I heard a holy one speaking, and another holy one said to him, "How long will it take for the vision to be fulfilled—the vision concerning the daily sacrifice, the rebellion that causes desolation, and the surrender of the sanctuary and of the host that will be trampled underfoot?" He said to me, "It will take 2,300 evenings and mornings; then the sanctuary will be reconsecrated."
>
> Daniel 8:13–14

The rebellion that causes desolation (the abomination of desolation) refers to the desecration of the altar in the temple at Jerusalem. Antiochus creates an altar to Zeus over the Jewish altar and offers unclean animals (pigs) as sacrifices on the altar. The text predicts that this desolation would last 2,300 days. This is approximately six years. Antiochus begins his desolation in 171 B.C., and in 165 B.C. the temple is cleansed and Jewish sacrifices restored.

Antiochus's brazen defiance of God and Jewish religion creates a rebellion that finally brings his own downfall. It is called the Maccabean Revolt. The story of this rebellion is recorded in the Book of Maccabees.

In those days Mattathias son of John, son of Simeon, a priest of the line of Joarib, left Jerusalem and settled in Modein. He had five sons, John known as Gaddi, Simon called Thassi, Judas called Maccabaeus, Eleazar, called Avaran, and Jonathan called Apphus. When he saw the blasphemies being committed in Judah and Jerusalem, he said, "Alas that I should have been born to witness the overthrow of my people, and the overthrow of the Holy City, and to sit by while she is delivered over to her enemies, and the sanctuary into the hand of foreigners.

"Her Temple has become like a man of no repute,
the vessels that were her glory have been carried off as booty,
her babies have been slaughtered in her streets,
her young men by the enemy's sword.
Is there a nation that has not claimed a share of her royal prerogatives,
that has not taken some of her spoils?
All her ornaments have been snatched from her,
her former freedom has become slavery.
See how our Holy Place, our beauty, our glory, is now laid waste,
profaned by the pagans.
What have we left to live for?"

Mattathias and his sons tore their garments, put on sackcloth, and observed deep mourning.

The king's commissioners who were enforcing the apostasy came to the town of Modein to make them sacrifice. Many Israelites gathered round them, but Mattathias and his sons drew apart. The king's commissioners then addressed Mattathias as follows, "You are a respected leader, a great man in this town; you have sons and brothers to support you. Be the first to step forward and conform to the king's decree, as all the nations have done, and the leaders of Judah and the survivors in Jerusalem; you and your sons shall be reckoned among the Friends of the King, you and your sons shall be honoured with gold and silver and many presents." Raising his voice, Mattathias retorted, "Even if every nation living in the king's dominions obeys him, each forsaking its ancestral religion to conform to his decrees, I, my sons and my brothers will still follow the covenant of our ancestors. Heaven preserve us from forsaking the Law and its observances. As for the king's orders, we will not follow them: we will not swerve from our own religion either to right or to left." As he finished speaking, a Jew came forward in the sight of all to offer sacrifice on the altar in Modein as the royal edict required. When Mattathias saw this, he was fired with zeal; stirred to the depth of his being, he gave vent to his legitimate anger, threw himself on the man and slaughtered him on the altar. At the same time he killed the king's commissioner who was there to enforce the sacrifice, and tore down the altar. In his zeal for the Law he acted as Phinehas did against Zimri son of Salu. Then Mattathias went through the town, shouting at the top of his voice, "Let everyone who has a fervour for the Law and takes his stand on the covenant come out and follow me." Then he fled with his sons into the hills, leaving all their possessions behind in the town.

1 Maccabees 2:1–28 JB

Shortly after this event, Mattathias died. His son Judas forms a band of guerrilla fighters. Judas is called "the hammer," and his tactics lead to the downfall of Antiochus. Although Antiochus has 100,000 foot soldiers, 20,000 cavalry, and 32 elephants, he is no match for Judas and his guerrillas. Antiochus is forced back to Syria. Demetrius, who is the rightful king of Syria and has been released from prison in Rome, is now on the throne. He arrests Antiochus and has him beheaded.

On December 25, 165 B.C., the temple is rededicated. An eight-day celebration is called. On the first day they light a candle. On the second day a second candle, etc. This is now called the feast of Hanukkah.

History Repeats Itself

While I, Daniel, was watching the vision and trying to understand it, there before me stood one who looked like a man. And I heard a man's voice from the Ulai calling, "Gabriel, tell this man the meaning of the vision."

As he came near the place where I was standing, I was terrified and fell prostrate. "Son of man," he said to me, "understand that the vision concerns the time of the end."

While he was speaking to me, I was in a deep sleep, with my face to the ground. Then he touched me and raised me to my feet.

He said, "I am going to tell you what will happen later in the time of wrath, because the vision concerns the appointed time of the end. The two-horned ram that you saw represents the kings of Media and Persia. The shaggy goat is the king of Greece, and the large horn between his eyes is the first king. The four horns that replaced the one that was broken off represent four kingdoms that will emerge from his nation but will not have the same power.

"In the latter part of their reign, when rebels have become completely wicked, a stern-faced king, a master of intrigue, will arise. He will become very strong, but not by his own power. He will cause astounding devastation and will succeed in whatever he does. He will destroy the mighty men and the holy people. He will cause deceit to prosper, and he will consider himself superior. When they feel secure, he will destroy many and take his stand against the Prince of princes. Yet he will be destroyed, but not by human power.

"The vision of the evenings and mornings that has been given you is true, but seal up the vision, for it concerns the distant future."

I, Daniel, was exhausted and lay ill for several days. Then I got up and went about the king's business. I was appalled by the vision; it was beyond understanding.

Daniel 8:15–27

Antiochus Epiphanes is a prototype of the Antichrist. Now the final master of intrigue is described. Note some of the unusual characteristics. He will become strong, but not by his own power. This probably refers to the power of Satan. He will persecute the holy people. He will elevate himself to God. He will desecrate the temple. He will be destroyed, but not by human power. This refers to divine intervention—the coming of Christ.

There are a number of prophetic events that we have discussed so far from the writings of Daniel. At the end of the world there will be a revival of the Roman Empire—a political and economic coalition. Out of that coalition, Antichrist will come in the spirit of Antiochus Epiphanes. He will ultimately elevate himself as God. He will desecrate the temple. He will offer pagan sacrifices in Jerusalem and the temple. Then Christ will come and destroy Antichrist. For all of this to occur, there are at least two historical prerequisites:

1. *Israel must exist as a nation.* For Antichrist to come on the scene, it is necessary for Israel to be a nation-state, because he will form a coalition with the nation of Israel. In the year A.D. 70 Jerusalem was sacked.

The temple was destroyed. The Jews were dispersed across the world. For nearly two thousand years they lived separated from their land. But in the late 1940s Israel, for the first time in almost two thousand years, became a nation-state.

2. *There must be a political coalition that rises out of the ancient Roman Empire.* The European Common Market is renewing that empire in the form of economic cooperation. This reality has been expanded to include not only Western Europe, but Eastern Europe as well. It is out of that coalition that Antichrist will come.

Am I saying that we are in the endtimes? I am not a prophet. I am simply saying that the Bible predicts that at the end of time Israel will be a nation and there will be a revived coalition in Europe out of which Antichrist will come. What I am saying is that this is the first time since Jesus Christ ascended to heaven and Jerusalem was destroyed that these two factors are a reality. There is no prophecy that yet remains to be fulfilled before Jesus Christ would come. I believe that it is entirely possible the Antichrist could be alive on planet earth. Now Jesus Christ may tarry another hundred years or another thousand years, but what is exciting to me is that for the first time since he promised he would come again, all of the events of human history, as complex as they are, seem to be moving into place.

Insight

1. *Life is uncertain, but God is in control.* Daniel is disturbed by this vision. It seems beyond understanding (see Dan. 8:27). Daniel is an official in the Babylonian Empire. This is an empire that seems indestructible. God reveals to Daniel events of the future. He says, "Daniel, I'm about to show you things to come. That tiny, insignificant province over two hundred miles east of you will grow. It will dominate not only Persia, but also Babylon. Moreover, to the west in Greece, a ruler will come with lightning speed. He will conquer the world, and in the height of his power he will be cut off and the kingdom divided."

Daniel is confused: "Lord, you must be kidding. There is no way that those events can come to pass." Tomorrow is uncertain, but God is in control. The one thing I see in this passage is the uncertainty of life. The uncertainty of the future. The uncertainty of tomorrow. But underneath the uncertainty, the absolute assurance that God himself is in control.

God's larger purpose is demonstrated in both Medo-Persia and Greece. The Medo-Persian Empire begins with Cyrus the Great. What was God's larger purpose in bringing this man to the center stage of world influence? The answer to this question is found in the Book of Ezra.

> In the first year of Cyrus king of Persia, in order to fulfill the word of the LORD spoken by Jeremiah, the LORD moved the heart of Cyrus king of Persia to make a proclamation throughout his realm and to put it in writing:
>
> "This is what Cyrus king of Persia says:
> "'The LORD, the God of heaven, has given me all the kingdoms of the earth and he has appointed me to build a temple for him at Jerusalem in Judah. Anyone of his people among you—may his God be with him, and let him go up to Jerusalem in Judah and build the temple of the LORD, the God of Israel, the God who is in Jerusalem. And the people of any place where survivors may now be living are to provide him with silver and gold, with goods and livestock, and with freewill offerings for the temple of God in Jerusalem.'"
>
> Ezra 1:1–4

God used Cyrus to enable the Jews to return to their land.

God also had a larger purpose for Alexander the Great. Alexander brought the Greek language and culture to all the nations he conquered. For the first time in history people shared a common language—Greek. God used this common language for the writing of the New Testament and gave the world his revelation in the language they could understand. This language also simplified the spread of Christianity through a single common language. Life may be uncertain, but God is in control. He uses the circumstances of life to contribute to his greater purposes.

> And we know that in all things God works for the good of those who love him, who have been called according to his purpose. For those God foreknew he also predestined to be conformed to the likeness of his Son, that he might be the firstborn among many brothers.
>
> Romans 8:28–29

2. *There is one Antichrist, but there are many antichrists.* There is only one Antichrist (capital *A*) who will appear on the stage of human history. But there are many antichrists (lowercase *a*).

Dear children, this is the last hour; and as you have heard that the antichrist is coming, even now many antichrists have come. This is how we know it is the last hour.

1 John 2:18

Apparently there were people in the first century who made a commitment to Jesus Christ as Savior, but after a period of time they made choices in their lives that did not recognize Christ as the Lord of their life. In other words, they made choices that were not pro-Christ but rather antichrist. After a period of time of disobeying God, of making antichrist choices, the Bible says they eventually left the faith. They fell away.

Who are the antichrists today? They are people who make a commitment to Jesus Christ. They accept him, but they never recognize Christ's lordship in their life and behavior. Their attitudes, their thinking, their choices, and their relationships are not pro-Christ—they are antichrist. You see, you cannot make a genuine commitment to Christ and go out and live whatever way you want. Part of what it means to make a commitment to Jesus is not only to accept him but to live for him. It is possible to go to church, believe in Jesus, get baptized, be outwardly religious, and be a small antichrist. You are either for Christ in your lifestyle or against Christ. And if you are against Christ, you are an antichrist.

Who is the liar? It is the man who denies that Jesus is the Christ. Such a man is the antichrist—he denies the Father and the Son.

1 John 2:22

Other people are antichrist because they deny who Jesus is. Some say, "Well, I've heard about Jesus. I've listened to what you say. But Jesus is not for me. I reject the reality of Jesus and what he wants to do in my life." John says such a person is an antichrist. Let me draw the line and suggest this principle. When it comes to Jesus, you are either for him or you are against him. There is no neutral ground. You are either for Christ or you are against Christ. There are only two kingdoms here on this earth: the kingdom of Christ and the kingdom of Satan. There are only two fathers: God the Father or Satan the father. There is no middle ground. There is no mushy, gray middle. The Bible declares, Jesus is the Christ, the Son of God. He died. He was buried. He rose again. He is the Lord of history and the Christ of salvation. My choice is simple, I am either for him or against him.

Prayer

He who testifies to these things says, "Yes, I am coming soon."
Amen. Come, Lord Jesus.
The grace of the Lord Jesus be with God's people. Amen.

Revelation 22:20–21

Dear Lord, in the face of the darkness of the world in which we live, we long for the light of your coming. Even so, come Lord Jesus. Even so, come TODAY! Amen.

Chapter Thirteen

A Comprehensive Overview of the Endtimes

Daniel 9:24–27

Most dispensational interpreters of Bible prophecy would agree that Daniel 9:24–27 contains some of the most significant prophetic verses in the entire Bible. I would add that they are also some of the most difficult and confusing. How we interpret these verses determines our understanding of the events at the end of the world. How we interpret these verses determines our understanding of how and when the Lord will return. How we interpret these verses determines our understanding of the role of Israel in future events. Finally, how we interpret these verses determines whether we accept the church as the spiritual extension of Israel or whether Israel and the church are separate institutions in the economy of God.

The Decree of Jewish History

Seventy "sevens" are decreed for your people and your holy city to finish transgression, to put an end to sin, to atone for wickedness, to bring in everlasting righteousness, to seal up vision and prophecy and to anoint the most holy.

Daniel 9:24

165

This opening verse of the prophecy identifies a decree about Jewish history. There are three things about this decree that merit our attention: the length of time, the people involved, and the program of God.

The Length of Time

The text begins, "Seventy 'sevens' are decreed for your people and your holy city" (9:24). The Hebrew word translated "seven" is a word used to designate a unit of time divided into seven segments. The unit could be hours, days, weeks, months, years, or another period of time. The text is referring to seventy units of time (seventy sevens). Each unit is divided into seven segments.

I believe that these units refer to years. If this is true, then the text is referring to seventy units of seven years, or 490 years. I believe this is true for two reasons. First, the chapter begins by referring to seventy years.

> In the first year of Darius son of Xerxes (a Mede by descent), who was made ruler over the Babylonian kingdom—in the first year of his reign, I, Daniel, understood from the Scriptures, according to the word of the LORD given to Jeremiah the prophet, that the desolation of Jerusalem would last seventy years.
>
> Daniel 9:1–2

The chapter begins by referring to a time period of seventy years. Not days, weeks, or months. Years. It would make sense to carry this literal interpretation to the end of the chapter and conclude that the second seventy also refers to years. Second, the Jews were accustomed to the concept of a week of years or seven years. They spoke of the sabbatical year—the seventh year. For these two reasons, I believe that the seventy sevens refers to seventy units of seven years—490 years.

The People Involved

The text states that the people included in this decree are "your people and your holy city" (9:24). Daniel's people were the Jews, and his holy city was Jerusalem. So the prophecy deals with the Jewish people and the city of Jerusalem. This is a significant shift in the focus of the prophecies of Daniel. All previous prophecies have dealt with the Gentiles, not the Jews.

The two-horned ram that you saw represents the kings of Media and Persia. The shaggy goat is the king of Greece, and the large horn between his eyes is the first king.

Daniel 8:20–21

In chapters 7 and 8 there are many prophecies recorded, and all of them deal exclusively with the Gentile nations: the Babylonians, the Medes, the Persians, the Greeks, and the Romans. Now in chapter 9 the focus is exclusively on Israel and the holy city.

Seventy "sevens" are decreed for your people and your holy city to finish transgression, to put an end to sin, to atone for wickedness, to bring in everlasting righteousness, to seal up vision and prophecy and to anoint the most holy.

Daniel 9:24

The word *decreed* means "to decide something, to determine something, or to cut something out." Let me paraphrase the opening statement. God has cut 490 years out of human history to accomplish a specific purpose with Israel and Jerusalem. This is the introduction to the rest of the passage. God has set a specific period of time, which appears to be 490 years, in which he will accomplish and bring to fulfillment his purpose, his plan, and his program. This is not for the Gentiles. It is not for the Romans. It is not for the Greeks. It is not for the Medes. It is not for the Persians or the Babylonians. It is for Israel and Jerusalem.

The Program of God

There are six things listed that God is going to do during this 490-year period of time. The first three were accomplished through the coming of Christ to suffer, die, and rise again. The last three will be accomplished when Christ returns the second time. These six things are as follows:

1. finish transgression
2. put an end to sin
3. atone for wickedness
4. bring in everlasting righteousness
5. seal up the vision (close the pages on human history)
6. anoint the most holy (consecrate the temple)

The Divisions of Jewish History

Daniel 9:25–27 gives the breakdown of the "seventy sevens." Three separate time periods are identified.

1. Seven "sevens" (v. 25). This would be 7 x 7 years or 49 years.
2. Sixty-two "sevens" (v. 26). This would be 62 x 7 years or 434 years.
3. One "seven" (v. 27). This would be 1 x 7 years or 7 years.

The 490-year span of time is divided into three time periods. The first is forty-nine years. The second is 434 years. The last is seven years. In the text, the first two time periods go together and deal with the rebuilding of Jerusalem and the coming of the Messiah.

Predictions about the Coming Messiah

Know and understand this: From the issuing of the decree to restore and rebuild Jerusalem until the Anointed One, the ruler, comes, there will be seven "sevens," and sixty-two "sevens." It will be rebuilt with streets and a trench, but in times of trouble. After the sixty-two "sevens," the Anointed One will be cut off and will have nothing.

Daniel 9:25–26

The first prediction states that from the "issuing of the decree to restore and rebuild Jerusalem until the Anointed One" (v. 25) there will be a total of 483 years (49 years and 434 years). In seeking to understand this prediction, it is important to identify which decree the text is referring to. There were actually three decrees given to promote the rebuilding of Jerusalem.

The Decree of Cyrus (538 B.C.)

In the first year of Cyrus king of Persia, in order to fulfill the word of the LORD spoken by Jeremiah, the LORD moved the heart of Cyrus king of Persia to make a proclamation throughout his realm and to put it in writing:

"This is what Cyrus king of Persia says:
"'The LORD, the God of heaven, has given me all the kingdoms of the earth and he has appointed me to build a temple for him at Jerusalem in Judah.'"

Ezra 1:1–2

This first decree deals primarily with the rebuilding of the temple. Although they rebuilt their houses and part of the city of Jerusalem, the intent of the decree was focused on the temple.

The Decree of Artaxerxes (458 B.C.)

This is a copy of the letter King Artaxerxes had given to Ezra the priest and teacher, a man learned in matters concerning the commands and decrees of the LORD for Israel:

... With this money be sure to buy bulls, rams and male lambs, together with their grain offerings and drink offerings, and sacrifice them on the altar of the temple of your God in Jerusalem.

Ezra 7:11, 17

This second decree dealt primarily with the restoration of worship at the rebuilt temple.

The Decree of Artaxerxes (445 B.C.)

The king said to me, "What is it you want?"

Then I prayed to the God of heaven, and I answered the king, "If it pleases the king and if your servant has found favor in his sight, let him send me to the city in Judah where my fathers are buried so that I can rebuild it."

Then the king, with the queen sitting beside him, asked me, "How long will your journey take, and when will you get back?" It pleased the king to send me; so I set a time.

Nehemiah 2:4–6

This third decree deals exclusively with the rebuilding of the city of Jerusalem—not the temple or its worship. This is most likely the decree referred to in the prophecy of Daniel (9:25). This would date the decree at 445 B.C. From this date until the Messiah comes will be 483 years. More precisely, there will be 483 years until Messiah is "cut off and will have nothing" (9:26). This is a reference to the death of the Anointed and the fact that he does not establish an earthly kingdom.

When you subtract the 483 years from 445 B.C. you come up with the date A.D. 38. This is a problem. Since Jesus died when he was thirty-three (A.D. 33), the dates are off by five years. However, this apparent discrepancy can be resolved. The Jewish calendar is different than our calendar. The Jewish calendar is built on lunar years, and it has only 360 days. Our calendar is built on solar years, and there are 365 days. If you are into math, you can crunch the numbers yourself. When you take the difference between our year and the Jewish year and factor that into the sixty-nine weeks (483 years), you will come up with the year A.D. 33! The prediction is exact to the year.

The Last Week

> The people of the ruler who will come will destroy the city and the sanctuary. The end will come like a flood: War will continue until the end, and desolations have been decreed. He will confirm a covenant with many for one "seven." In the middle of the "seven" he will put an end to sacrifice and offering. And on a wing of the temple he will set up an abomination that causes desolation, until the end that is decreed is poured out on him.
>
> Daniel 9:26–27

This second part of the prediction begins by stating that "the people of the ruler who will come will destroy the city and the sanctuary" (v. 26). Who is this ruler? First, it is not Jesus Christ. He already came and was "cut off" (v. 26). Second, these people will destroy the city (Jerusalem) and the sanctuary (the temple). This would mean that they are the enemies of God. Third, the rest of the prediction seems to refer to the ruler as the Antichrist. Antichrist operates in this last seven-year span of time (see Dan. 9:27).

If this last period of time follows consecutively after the first sixty-nine periods of time, then the predicted authority of Antichrist would have already occurred immediately following the death of Christ. From our vantage point of history we know that this is not what happened.

What then does this prediction mean? Let me suggest that between the sixty-ninth week and the seventieth week there is a parenthesis in human history. This is a period of time not dealt with in this prophecy. It is the time period in which we are now living—the Church Age. But you may well ask, "If God knew about the church, why did he not throw it into the prophecy as well?" This is a legitimate question.

The answer to this question lies in understanding that the concept of the church was a mystery throughout the Old Testament.

For this reason I, Paul, the prisoner of Christ Jesus for the sake of you Gentiles—

Surely you have heard about the administration of God's grace that was given to me for you, that is, the mystery made known to me by revelation, as I have already written briefly. In reading this, then, you will be able to understand my insight into the mystery of Christ, which was not made known to men in other generations as it has now been revealed by the Spirit to God's holy apostles and prophets. This mystery is that through the gospel the Gentiles are heirs together with Israel, members together of one body, and sharers together in the promise in Christ Jesus.

Ephesians 3:1–6

The mystery of the church was something that people before Paul did not understand. It was a complete mystery. Daniel did not understand it. Jeremiah did not understand it. Isaiah did not understand it. The minor prophets did not understand it. No one understood it! What was that mystery? The mystery was that there would come a time in God's dealing with humanity when the distinction of Jew and Gentile would be irrelevant. God would extend his grace to everyone—Jew and Gentile alike. Together they would *all* be partakers of Jesus Christ. No male or female. No Jew or Gentile. No bond or free. All one in Christ. Therefore it would have violated this mystery if God had clearly revealed it to Daniel in this incredible prophecy.

God says to Daniel, "I'm going to reveal to you my purpose for Israel and for Jerusalem. I am cutting out of history 490 years to deal with Israel and with Jerusalem. After the first sixty-nine weeks (483 years), Messiah will be crucified. Then at the end of time I will return again to my people Israel in the seventieth week (another seven years). Antichrist will come. Certain things will happen, and then I will return in glory." "Okay, God," Daniel says, "what about in between?" God says, "Daniel, I can't tell you. It's a mystery. It's an unbelievable thing that I have in mind." Thank God that you and I live in the parenthesis between the crucifixion and the second coming.

The Tribulation Period

He will confirm a covenant with many for one "seven." In the middle of the "seven" he will put an end to sacrifice and offering. And on a wing of the temple he will set up an abomination that causes desolation, until the end that is decreed is poured out on him.

Daniel 9:27

Antichrist will do three things in the last seven years.

1. He will confirm a covenant for seven years.
2. In the middle of the seven years, he will put an end to sacrifice and offering.
3. He will set up the abomination that causes desolation in the wing of the temple.

The key phrases in understanding this prophecy are the "abomination that causes desolation" (v. 27), and the idea of three and a half years between the stopping of sacrifice in the temple and the abomination. The prophecy implies that Antichrist will forge a peace alliance with Israel for seven years. In the middle of that time period, he will violate the agreement and stop the temple worship. He will go further and desecrate the temple in the spirit of Antiochus Epiphanes (see Dan. 8:25). This same prophecy is repeated later in the Book of Daniel, and the time period is 1,290 days, or three and a half years.

From the time that the daily sacrifice is abolished and the abomination that causes desolation is set up, there will be 1,290 days.

Daniel 12:11

The Book of Revelation also talks about this three and a half year time span of blasphemy by Antichrist.

The beast was given a mouth to utter proud words and blasphemies and to exercise the authority for forty-two months. He opened his mouth to blaspheme God, and to slander his name and his dwelling place and those who live in heaven. He was given power to make war against the saints and to conquer them. And he was given authority over every tribe, people, language and nation. All inhabitants of the earth will worship the beast— all whose names have not been written in the book of life belonging to the Lamb that was slain from the creation of the world.

Revelation 13:5-9

Jesus speaks of the abomination of desolation as one of the events prior to his return to earth.

> So when you see standing in the holy place "the abomination that causes desolation," spoken of through the prophet Daniel—let the reader understand—then let those who are in Judea flee to the mountains. Let no one on the roof of his house go down to take anything out of the house. Let no one in the field go back to get his cloak. How dreadful it will be in those days for pregnant women and nursing mothers! Pray that your flight will not take place in winter or on the Sabbath. For then there will be great distress, unequaled from the beginning of the world until now—and never to be equaled again.
>
> Matthew 24:15–21

> At that time the sign of the Son of Man will appear in the sky, and all the nations of the earth will mourn. They will see the Son of Man coming on the clouds of the sky, with power and great glory. And he will send his angels with a loud trumpet call, and they will gather his elect from the four winds, from one end of the heavens to the other.
>
> Matthew 24:30–31

All of these prophecies refer to the last seven years prior to the coming of Christ. It will be a time of desolation and suffering. The temple will be devastated. The agreement made by Antichrist will be broken. But Christ will come to defeat Antichrist and his forces.

Where Is the Church?

Four hundred and ninety years divided into three time periods. After forty-nine years Jerusalem is rebuilt. The Old Testament prophecy is completed. Sixty weeks (420 years) later, at the sixty-ninth week (483rd year), Messiah comes and in the year A.D. 33 is crucified. He dies on the cross. There is a parenthesis in which God extends his grace to people worldwide. But at the end of time he will return again to the nation of Israel and the city of Jerusalem.

Before Messiah returns, Antichrist will arrive upon the scene and form a coalition with Israel for seven years. In the middle of the seven years, he will break that covenant. He will bring about the abomination of desolation, and *then* it happens! God closes the envelope of history as we know it. He seals the vision and says to the saints, "Folks, it's time to go back down." In glory, majesty, and power Christ returns.

Question: In this last seven-year time period, where is the church? What is obvious from studying the record of prophecy—the church is not mentioned. It is not there. So what happened to it? We have this parenthesis between the sixty-ninth week (483rd year and Christ's death) and the seventieth weeks (final seven-year period). The seventieth week starts—no church! Israel, Jerusalem, the Jews, Antichrist. But no church. The answer, I believe, is the rapture. Jesus will come in the clouds to receive the church into heaven. That will usher in the seventieth week, or the last seven years of tribulation. This time period will be dominated by Antichrist, who will persecute Israel and desecrate the temple. At the end of the seven years, Christ will return to establish His kingdom.

> Brothers, we do not want you to be ignorant about those who fall asleep, or to grieve like the rest of men, who have no hope. We believe that Jesus died and rose again and so we believe that God will bring with Jesus those who have fallen asleep in him. According to the Lord's own word, we tell you that we who are still alive, who are left till the coming of the Lord, will certainly not precede those who have fallen asleep. For the Lord himself will come down from heaven, with a loud command, with the voice of the archangel and with the trumpet call of God, and the dead in Christ will rise first. After that, we who are still alive and are left will be caught up together with them in the clouds to meet the Lord in the air. And so we will be with the Lord forever. Therefore encourage each other with these words.
>
> 1 Thessalonians 4:13–18

Insight

The suffering of Christ was not an accident of human history, it was according to the plan of God. The suffering of Christ and his death are predicted throughout the Old Testament, including the Book of Daniel. His death was not an accident, nor was he the victim of the changing whim of public opinion. He died because this was in the plan and purpose of God.

Prayer

Dear Lord, thank you for sending your Son into the world to suffer, die, and rise again. Lord Jesus, thank you for being our substitute. Holy Spirit, thank you for drawing me to Christ. Amen.

Chapter Fourteen

Confronted by Jesus

Daniel 10:1–21

The last three chapters of the Book of Daniel (10, 11, and 12) form a cohesive unit and relate to Daniel's final vision of future events. One commentator says of these chapters: "There is hardly anything in the Bible that is just like these chapters, especially like chapter eleven. The word, the vision, and minute predictions are combined in a manner that is found nowhere else in the Scriptures" (Herbert Carl Leupold, *Exposition of Daniel* [Grand Rapids: Baker Book House, 1969], 441). Chapter 10 is an introduction to the vision and the predictions that it contains.

The Condition of Daniel

In the third year of Cyrus king of Persia, a revelation was given to Daniel (who was called Belteshazzar). Its message was true and it concerned a great war. The understanding of the message came to him in a vision.

Daniel 10:1

The ninth chapter of Daniel contains a prayer. Daniel is reading from the prophet Jeremiah, and he discovers that God made a promise through the prophet. He promised that after seventy years of captivity in Babylon, he would regather the people of Israel back to Israel. The temple

175

would be rebuilt. The city would be rebuilt, and God would reconfirm his promise to the people of Israel.

Daniel knows that the seventy years is about up. So he begins to pray. He confesses his sin and the sins of the people. He asks for God's intervention to regather the exiles back into Palestine. Shortly after the prayer, Cyrus issues a decree that permits the Jews to return home. Under the leadership of Ezra, they go back to Palestine. Two years after the decree and the initial return, Daniel has the vision that is recorded in chapter 10. The vision concerned "a great war" (v. 1). This could be either an angelic war or a human war. We will discover that in this case it refers to both kinds of war. The word for *war* also means conflict and suffering. So Daniel's vision relates to a future of angelic and human war, of conflict and suffering.

> At the time I, Daniel, mourned for three weeks. I ate no choice food; no meat or wine touched my lips; and I used no lotions at all until the three weeks were over.
>
> Daniel 10:2–3

This is a most interesting response. Why would Daniel mourn and fast for three weeks? After all, Ezra and many of the exiles had returned to Jerusalem. The altar of the temple is being rebuilt. The foundations of the temple are being strengthened. There is much to celebrate. But there is a problem. Shortly after the work commences, there is significant opposition. The work comes to a halt. Daniel probably receives the news that the work of rebuilding the temple has stopped. So in response to the bad news, Daniel mourns and fasts. In fact, he does two things:

1. He practices a partial fast. "I ate no choice food; no meat or wine touched my lips" (v. 3).
2. He uses no lotions. "I used no lotions at all until the three weeks were over" (v. 3).

Both these things are acts of humility before God. Their purpose is to help Daniel focus on God and gain wisdom from God.

> Then he continued, "Do not be afraid, Daniel. Since the first day that you set your mind to gain understanding and to humble yourself before your God, your words were heard, and I have come in response to them."
>
> Daniel 10:12

The Coming of Christ

Daniel is standing by the Tigris River outside the city of Babylon. He has a group of men with him and is most likely doing government business. He sees a man of distinctive features who leaves Daniel helpless and deathly pale (see Dan. 10:8). I believe that this man is none other than Jesus Christ. Daniel describes him.

His Fashion

> I looked up and there before me was a man dressed in linen, with a belt of the finest gold around his waist.
>
> Daniel 10:5

His dress implies the dress of priest, prophet, and king. The linen garment represents the clothing of a priest. The belt represents the clothing of a prophet. The gold represents the clothing of a king.

His Features

> His body was like chrysolite, his face like lightning, his eyes like flaming torches, his arms and legs like the gleam of burnished bronze, and his voice like the sound of a multitude.
>
> Daniel 10:6

This is certainly an imposing figure. His body is like chrysolite, which is a yellowish gold transparent stone. His face is like lightning. His eyes like flaming torches. His arms and legs like bronze. His voice is like the sound of a multitude.

This description of Christ is very similar to the one given in the Book of Revelation.

> I turned around to see the voice that was speaking to me. And when I turned I saw seven golden lampstands, and among the lampstands was someone "like a son of man," dressed in a robe reaching down to his feet and with a golden sash around his chest. His head and hair were white like wool, as white as snow, and his eyes were like blazing fire. His feet were like bronze glowing in a furnace, and his voice was like the sound of rushing waters. In his right hand he held seven stars, and out of his mouth came

a sharp double-edged sword. His face was like the sun shining in all its brilliance.

Revelation 1:12–16

Note the similarities:

Daniel 10:5–6	Revelation 1:12–16
dressed in linen	dressed in a robe
golden belt	golden sash
eyes like flaming torches	eyes like blazing fire
arms and legs gleaming like burnished bronze	feet like bronze glowing in a furnace
voice like the sound of a multitude	voice like the sound of rushing waters

There is no doubt that the person in the Book of Revelation is the glorified Christ. The context makes that clear. The incredible similarity between Daniel and Revelation leads one to conclude that both passages deal with the same person—Jesus Christ. The first passage (Daniel) is a preincarnate appearance of Christ. The second passage (Revelation) is a postglorification appearance of Christ.

Daniel's response to seeing this man is similar to John's response to seeing the resurrected and glorified Christ.

> I, Daniel, was the only one who saw the vision; the men with me did not see it, but such terror overwhelmed them that they fled and hid themselves. So I was left alone, gazing at this great vision; I had no strength left, my face turned deathly pale and I was helpless. Then I heard him speaking, and as I listened to him, I fell into a deep sleep, my face to the ground.
>
> Daniel 10:7–9

When John saw Christ in all his glory, the text states that he "fell at his feet as though dead" (Rev. 1:17). Isaiah had a similar response when he saw the Lord (see Isa. 6:1–5).

The Cosmic Conflict

> Then he continued, "Do not be afraid, Daniel. Since the first day that you set your mind to gain understanding and to humble yourself before your

God, your words were heard, and I have come in response to them. But the
prince of the Persian kingdom resisted me twenty-one days. Then Michael,
one of the chief princes, came to help me, because I was detained there
with the king of Persia. Now I have come to explain to you what will happen to your people in the future, for the vision concerns a time yet to come."

Daniel 10:12–14

Let me paraphrase this unusual set of circumstances. An angelic messenger comes to Daniel and says, "God has heard your prayer. I have
come to give you an answer. I am sorry that I am a little late. I was detained
along the way. In fact, I ran into stiff opposition. Had it not been for the
help of Michael, one of the chief angels of heaven, I might still be involved
in this resistance."

Several facts are obvious. First, it is obvious that this ruler, whoever
it is, is associated with the Persian kingdom. This prince connected with
the kingdom is resisting the will of God. God has sent an angel to bring
a message to Daniel, and this prince assigned to Persia is deliberately
resisting and opposing God. It is also obvious that this prince of the Persian kingdom has significant power—supernatural power. Power bigger
than human power because it requires Michael, one of the chief princes
of heaven, to defeat this Persian power.

I think the only logical interpretation is that this prince of Persia is one
of Satan's demons. Stronger than a human being. Stronger than a human
ruler. A demon assigned by Satan to Persia for the express purpose of
opposing and resisting the will of God in the kingdom of Persia.

This is one of the very few passages in the Bible that gives a glimpse
into the spirit world and describes the conflict between Satan and God's
angels. The other significant passage on this topic is in the New Testament.

For our struggle is not against flesh and blood, but against the rulers, against
the authorities, against the powers of this dark world and against the spiritual forces of evil in the heavenly realms.

Ephesians 6:12

The battle is not merely physical. It is spiritual. It is a battle against
Satan and his legions of demons who are active in the world in which we
live. There are several factors about Satan and spiritual warfare that are
worth noting from Daniel's vision.

1. *Satan is alive and well.* Spiritual conflict in the heavenly realm is real. The demons and the angels are doing battle.

2. *Satan assigned demons to two nations.* The passage in Daniel talks about the prince of Persia (10:13) and the prince of Greece (10:20). Some speculate from this passage that Satan assigns demons to all countries and all organizations within those countries. For example, they would say that there is one demon assigned to the United States, another assigned to Michigan, one assigned to Grand Rapids, and still others assigned to the various organizations in Grand Rapids. All we can be sure of from this text is that one was assigned to Persia and another to Greece. To carry this beyond the text is to be extrabiblical—not unbiblical.

3. *Daniel was unaware of this conflict and did not participate in it.* This battle between Michael and the prince of Persia happened without Daniel's knowledge. Moreover, Daniel did *not* participate in its outcome. Is warfare in the spirit realm for real? Yes. Do we participate in it? No.

The angel who came to Daniel had an objective in mind.

> So he said, "Do you know why I have come to you? Soon I will return to fight against the prince of Persia, and when I go, the prince of Greece will come; but first I will tell you what is written in the Book of Truth. (No one supports me against them except Michael, your prince. And in the first year of Darius the Mede, I took my stand to support and protect him.)"
>
> Daniel 10:20–11:1

Insight

1. *In a culture of excess, self-denial demonstrates our humility before God.* Daniel went on a partial fast to illustrate his humility before God. I think that we as believers have forgotten that part of the call of commitment to Christ is self-denial. Jesus said that part of following him is self-denial. You know what that means? It means saying *no* to self. Saying *no* to our desires. Saying *no* to the flesh. Saying *no* to pleasure. Paul says the same thing.

> Therefore I do not run like a man running aimlessly; I do not fight like a man beating the air. No, I beat my body and make it my slave so that after I have preached to others, I myself will not be disqualified for the prize.
>
> 1 Corinthians 9:26–27

In writing to Timothy, Paul outlines the qualifications for spiritual leadership (see 1 Tim. 3). Two of the requirements are temperance and self-control. Whatever happened to fasting? To frugality? To simplicity? To restraint? Whatever happened to the idea of saying *no* to self? Not as a means of grace. Not as a way to earn our salvation. Not a physical putting down of the body. But practicing self-denial. In a culture of excess, of money and material things, of television, food, and pleasure, who will dare to say no?

I grew up in the '60s. I am a product of '60s thinking. Like many people my age in the church, I grew up in an evangelical environment that was highly structured. Lots of rules. Lots of regulations. That's the way I grew up. You could not grow your hair long. No smoking. No drinking. No going to movies. No television on Sunday. No sports on Sunday. No eating in a restaurant on Sunday. The danger in all of that was to equate not going to movies with being committed to Christ. Those who obeyed all of the rules and fit into the box were more spiritual than those who did not.

My generation came along, and we rejected many of those rules and regulations. We allowed our children to do things that we were not allowed to do. After all, as many of my friends say, "We are not legalists. We don't want to be legalistic. I don't want to have all of these rules. I don't want all of these things that fit in a box. After all, there is liberty and freedom in Christ!" And thank God there *is* liberty and freedom in Jesus Christ. We are not going to be judged by "touch not, taste not, handle not" (see Col. 2:21). We've been set free! But the struggle I sense is that in our freedom from the rules we have a tendency to go all the way to excess with no restraint. There is no self-denial. There is indulgence.

I am convinced that one of the paths to spiritual godly character is a path that understands on the one hand I am absolutely free in Jesus Christ, but on the other hand I will not allow my freedom in Christ to hinder my progress or to hurt others. There will be significant choices in my own personal life whereby I will say, "No, that's enough." Excess! In a culture of excess, God demands self-restraint in how we spend our money. Self-restraint in how we eat. Self-restraint in the programs we watch on television. Self-restraint in every area of our life. I think one of the reasons Daniel was such a person of God in a pagan culture is that although he was free, he voluntarily made some significant choices that demonstrate self-restraint.

2. *Be careful about your attitude toward Satan.* There are at least three important principles in regard to our response to Satan and spirit conflict.

Beware of an overemphasis on Satan and demons. Beware of continually studying and worrying about Satan. Beware of making Satan and demons the central focus of your thinking and Christian life. Remember, Satan cannot harm the believer.

> We know that anyone born of God does not continue to sin; the one who was born of God keeps him safe, and the evil one cannot harm him.
>
> 1 John 5:18

Beware of an underemphasis on Satan and demons. To ignore Satan and demons is to ignore clear spiritual realities. Satan is alive. Demons do work. We are warned to watch out for Satan and his devices.

> Be self-controlled and alert. Your enemy the devil prowls around like a roaring lion looking for someone to devour. Resist him, standing firm in the faith, because you know that your brothers throughout the world are undergoing the same kind of sufferings.
>
> 1 Peter 5:8–9

Put on the armor of God and resist the devil. The insight from Daniel's experience is that this spirit conflict occurred without his knowledge or participation. There was no binding of Satan or deliverance prayers. It all happened apart from Daniel. Our responsibility is to put on the armor, stand fast in the faith, pray, and resist the devil (see Eph. 6:10–17; James 4:7; 1 Peter 5:8–9).

Prayer

> Submit yourselves, then, to God. Resist the devil, and he will flee from you.
>
> James 4:7

Dear God, I yield my life to you. Take my mind. Take my ears. Take my eyes. Take my tongue. Take my hands. Take my feet. Take me completely. Fill me with your Spirit. Help me to live in submission to you so that when Satan comes I may resist him in your strength. Amen.

Chapter Fifteen

God and the History of War

Daniel 11:1–35

Anyone can be a prophet after the fact! I predict that the United States will defeat Iraq in Desert Storm. I predict that Governor Bill Clinton of Arkansas will become president of the United States. I predict that the Berlin Wall will come down. I predict that the Chicago Bulls will win three back-to-back NBA titles. I predict that the Dallas Cowboys will win the Super Bowl in 1993. I predict. . . . These are easy to predict because they are events that have already taken place.

Future Historical Events

The eleventh chapter of Daniel contains some striking and detailed prophecies about future historical events. In the first part of this chapter (vv. 1–35), there are 135 prophetic statements that have already been fulfilled in every historical detail. Some have called into question whether these details were written *before* the events happened or *after* the events happened. In the third century after Christ, a philosopher named Porphyry attacked the authority of these prophecies and concluded that they were a forgery. He claimed that since all the detailed events outlined in this prophecy did take place, they must have been written by someone after the events had occurred. In response to this attack, Jerome wrote a commentary defending the Book of Daniel as prophecy written hundreds of years before the predicted events took place.

The debate continues today. F. W. Farrar, a modern liberal, states in his book entitled *The Book of Daniel*, "If this chapter were indeed the utterance of a prophet in the Babylonian exile, namely 400 years before the events—events of which many are of small comparative importance in the world's history—which are here so minutely depicted, the revelation would be the most unique and perplexing in the whole Scriptures." Was this written before the events (in Babylonian exile) or during a later time when the events had already taken place (the Maccabean period)?

For years, liberal scholars, in their attempt to deny the supernatural content of prophetic Scripture, dated the Book of Daniel during the first century before Christ (the Maccabean period). This would ensure that the events predicted had already taken place. However, there is now considerable evidence to confirm that the Book of Daniel was *not* written during the Maccabean period, but rather several hundred years earlier. This would mean that all of the events were predicted before they happened. There is clear evidence to support this view.

The Dead Sea Scrolls

A number of years ago copies of the Old Testament were discovered in Palestine and were named the Dead Sea Scrolls. The Dead Sea Scrolls belong to a community of Jewish separatists who lived in the first and second centuries before Christ. They were committed to the preservation of the Law and the Scriptures. We are absolutely sure from archaeological evidence that these people living in the first and second centuries before Christ had copies of God's Word and that among those copies were parts of the Book of Daniel. Now scholars are relatively sure that these copies of the Old Testament date back to 400 to 500 B.C.—including the Book of Daniel.

Those who deny that Daniel wrote it suggest the Book of Daniel was actually written in the first century before Christ when all of the events in chapter 11 had already taken place. But with the dramatic discovery of these Dead Sea Scrolls, we can now date the Book of Daniel, not to the first century, because these people who lived prior to the first century already had a copy of Daniel, but rather we can now date the Book of Daniel during the Babylonian exile.

The Hebrew and Aramaic Texts

The style and content of both the Hebrew and Aramaic texts of Daniel suggest that it most closely parallels the Hebrew and Aramaic of the sixth century before Christ. It does *not* parallel the Hebrew and Aramaic language of the first century before Christ.

When you combine the evidence from the Dead Sea Scrolls and the evidence of language style, it makes sense to date the book during the Babylonian exile. This means that all the historical events mentioned in chapter 11 were predicted before any of them took place. But does it make any difference? Is it important to maintain the prophetic dimension of the Book of Daniel? The answer is *yes*, and there are two fundamental reasons why we must maintain the historicity and prophetic nature of the Book of Daniel.

1. *The integrity of Jesus.*

So when you see standing in the holy place "the abomination that causes desolation," spoken of through the prophet Daniel—let the reader understand. . . .

Matthew 24:15

For then there will be great distress, unequaled from the beginning of the world until now—and never to be equaled again.

Matthew 24:21

At that time the sign of the Son of Man will appear in the sky, and all the nations of the earth will mourn. They will see the Son of Man coming on the clouds of the sky, with power and great glory.

Matthew 24:30

These three verses are quotations by Jesus from the Book of Daniel (see Dan. 12:11; 12:1; 7:13). Jesus accepted these writings as prophetic. When you deny their prophetic importance by implying that they are part forgery, then you are calling into question the integrity of Jesus, who accepted these writings as prophetic.

2. *The supernatural element of Scripture.* When you explain away the supernatural—whether it be prophecy or miracles—you have eliminated the supernatural dimension of Scripture. The Bible is not an ordinary

book. It is God's supernatural revelation to human beings (see 2 Tim. 3:16–17; 2 Peter 1:21).

The Kings of Medo-Persia

Now then, I tell you the truth: Three more kings will appear in Persia, and then a fourth, who will be far richer than all the others. When he has gained power by his wealth, he will stir up everyone against the kingdom of Greece.

Daniel 11:2–3

Four kings are mentioned. The fourth king will be "richer than all the others" (v. 2). This king is Xerxes (486–465 B.C.). Xerxes' father was named Darius. In 490 B.C., Darius attacked Greece and suffered a humiliating defeat. When Xerxes comes to the throne, he is determined to avenge his father's defeat by the Greeks. He comes to power during a period of economic prosperity, and he uses his wealth to build an army. The military buildup lasts four and one-half years, until there are 2.5 million soldiers and twelve hundred ships. In 480 B.C. he launchs an expedition against Greece, but like his father, he is defeated and humiliated. He retreats to Persia. Historians mark this military defeat as the beginning of the end of the Persian Empire. Even though the empire lasted another 140 years, this military defeat was the watershed event in its decline.

Alexander the Great

Then a mighty king will appear, who will rule with great power and do as he pleases. After he has appeared, his empire will be broken up and parceled out toward the four winds of heaven. It will not go to his descendants, nor will it have the power he exercised, because his empire will be uprooted and given to others.

Daniel 11:3–4

The "mighty king" referred to in these verses is Alexander the Great. Four specific things are predicted about him.

1. He will rule with great power.
2. His kingdom will be divided into four parts.
3. His descendants will not assume power after his death.

4. The divided empire will not have the same power as the united empire under Alexander.

Alexander was born in the year 356 B.C. He ascends the Greek throne when he is twenty years old. He rules for thirteen years and dies at age thirty-three, after having conquered the entire world. Alexander has three sons: Philip, who is mentally handicapped; Alexander, who is born after his death; Hercules, who is an illegitimate son. When Alexander dies, his generals get together and appoint Philip and Alexander, two of his sons, as coregents of the Greek Empire. They are both children, so several people are appointed to make the decisions for the empire. But this does not last very long. There is intense argument among the generals and the leaders. As a result, Philip, Alexander, and Hercules are all murdered. The generals decide to divide this mighty empire into four sections, with a general ruling in each of those sections. These events follow the details of Daniel's prophecy. In fact, the predictions were made 216 years *before* the events happened.

The Divided Empire

The king of the South will become strong, but one of his commanders will become even stronger than he and will rule his own kingdom with great power. After some years, they will become allies. The daughter of the king of the South will go to the king of the North to make an alliance, but she will not retain her power, and he and his power will not last. In those days she will be handed over, together with her royal escort and her father and the one who supported her.

Daniel 11:5–6

The empire of Alexander is divided into four sections. These verses focus on two of those sections: the northern section (Syria) and the southern section (Egypt), with an emphasis on Palestine, which lies between these two countries. The king of the South is a man named Ptolemy Soter, one of Alexander's generals. When the kingdom is divided Ptolemy decides, "I will rule the southern part of the empire. I will take over Egypt and the surrounding area. I will become the king of the South." Seleucus Nicator, also one of the generals (a lesser general) and a subordinate to Ptolemy, decides, "I will stay in Babylon. I don't need an empire. I don't need a kingdom. I'll simply rule in this city." However, early in his reign he runs into conflict with another general (Antiochus), who drives Seleucus out of Babylon. He goes to Egypt and offers his services to Ptolemy. For a period of time this lesser general serves under Ptolemy in Egypt. Antiochus, who rules Babylon, is defeated. Seleucus then leaves Egypt, returns to Babylon, and becomes a mighty leader—even stronger than Ptolemy in the South (Egypt). In 304 B.C. both Ptolemy and Seleucus take on the title "king."

Fifty-four years pass. Ptolemy dies. His son, Ptolemy II, becomes the king of the South. Antiochus II Theos, the grandson of Seleucus, becomes the king of Babylon. Now stay with me. So you have Ptolemy II in Egypt, Antiochus in Babylon, and they are at war with each other. Finally they decide, "It's not good to fight each other. Let's make an alliance." Ptolemy offers his daughter, Bernice, to Antiochus as a wife. However, Antiochus is already married to a woman named Laodice. But he is so desperate for peace that he divorces Laodice and marries Bernice.

Two years after the marriage, Bernice's father, Ptolemy, dies. Apparently Antiochus is not well pleased with Bernice, so he decides to divorce Bernice and remarry his original wife, Laodice. However, Laodice is not a very forgiving person. Her motto is: "I may be dumb, but I ain't stupid." She does remarry him, but she poisons him. Laodice decides that Bernice was one of the chief causes of all of her troubles. Bernice, along with her royal escort, is headed back to Egypt. Laodice orders all of them killed. Now let us reread the verses that predict this.

> The king of the South [Ptolemy] will become strong, but one of his commanders [Seleucus] will become even stronger than he and will rule his own kingdom [Babylon] with great power. After some years [namely fifty-four] they will become allies. The daughter of the king of the South [Bernice] will go to the king of the North [Antiochus] to make an alliance, but she [Bernice] will not retain her power, and he [Antiochus] and his power will not last [he was poisoned]. In those days she [Bernice] will be handed over [murdered], together with her royal escort and her father [who has already died] and the one who supported her.
>
> Daniel 11: 5–6

These predictions were made about one hundred years before they happened.

Don't Get Mad—Get Even

The next several verses predict an ongoing conflict and hostility between the northern and southern pieces of the former Greek Empire. It is the story of revenge and revenge and revenge.

> One from her [this is referring to Bernice who has been killed by Laodice, who poisoned her husband] family—[in fact it's her brother, Ptolemy III] will arise to take her place [or literally to take up her cause—to get revenge]. He will attack the forces of the king of the North and enter his fortress [the capital, which is precisely what Ptolemy III did]; he will fight against them and be victorious [he has Laodice executed].
>
> Daniel 11:7

History records that when Ptolemy III marched north and defeated the Syrians (the northern kingdom) and killed Laodice that he returned to Egypt with over forty thousand talents of silver and twenty-five hundred vessels of gold.

> Then the king of the North will invade the realm of the king of the South but will retreat to his own country.
>
> Daniel 11:9

The king of the North mentioned here is Seleucus Callinicus. He decides to avenge the killing of Laodice. He sets out to invade Egypt, but his entire fleet is destroyed in a terrible storm. He returns home in humiliation and disgrace. His sons remember this defeat, and they set out to avenge their father's humiliation.

> His sons will prepare for war and assemble a great army, which will sweep on like an irresistible flood and carry the battle as far as his fortress.
>
> Daniel 11:10

The first son is Seleucus III, who reigns for four years and is killed in a battle in Asia Minor. The second son is Antiochus the Great. When he comes to power the Egyptians control as far north as the northern borders of Palestine. Antiochus the Great decides he is sick and tired of being in bondage to the Egyptians. So he gets a great army together and starts marching south. He conquers northern Palestine, central Palestine, and southern Palestine. He is all the way down to the desert that borders Egypt. Meanwhile, down in Egypt this is not received with joy.

> Then the king of the South will march out in a rage and fight against the king of the North, who will raise a large army, but it will be defeated.
>
> Daniel 11:11

The historical record indicates that this Egyptian king, Ptolemy Philopater, despised battle. He likes pleasure. He likes drink. He likes entertainment. He likes luxury. He despises conflict. But now he has had enough! Antiochus has marched down with this "irresistible flood." He has marched all the way to the borders of Egypt. So Ptolemy decides, "I have had enough. I don't want to fight. I don't like to fight. I don't enjoy fighting. But my survival is at stake." So he marches out with seventy thousand infantry, five thousand cavalry, and seventy-three elephants (ancient tanks with a trunk). Antiochus is at the border of Egypt with sixty-two thousand infantry, six thousand cavalry, and 103 elephants. They go to war. Antiochus is defeated. In fact, ten thousand of his soldiers are killed. Three hundred of his cavalry are killed. Five elephants are killed.

> When the army is carried off, the king of the South will be filled with pride and will slaughter many thousands, yet he will not remain triumphant.
>
> Daniel 11:12

Ptolemy Philopater defeats Antiochus the Great. But rather than pursuing him and totally devastating the army, he gets an initial victory and decides, "That's all I want. That's all I need. I'm going back down to Egypt. I'm going back down to enjoy the good life." This is a mistake, because Antiochus returns to his home and sets about strengthening his army for another attack (see Dan. 11:13).

The Exploits of Antiochus the Great

Verses 14–19 deal with the exploits of Antiochus the Great. They can be divided into two sections. First, his gaining control of Palestine. Second, his exploits with Egypt.

Gaining Control of Palestine

In those times many will rise against the king of the South [rebel against Egypt]. The violent men among your own people [remember this is written to Daniel, so it's speaking of the Jews] will rebel [against Egypt] in fulfillment of the vision, but without success. Then the king of the North [Antiochus the Great] will come and build up siege ramps and will capture a fortified city [Sidon]. The forces of the South will be powerless to resist; even their best troops will not have the strength to stand.

Daniel 11:14–15

Egypt sends its top three generals to intervene. They want to hold onto Sidon, but all of the wisdom and might of the Egyptians does not make a difference.

The invader will do as he pleases; no one will be able to stand against him. He will establish himself in the Beautiful Land and will have the power to destroy it.

Daniel 11:16

Exploits with Egypt

Antiochus sets his sights on the wealth and power of Egypt. He devises a plan to conquer Egypt.

He will determine to come with the might of his entire kingdom and will make an alliance with the king of the South. And he will give him a daughter in marriage [Cleopatra] in order to overthrow the kingdom, but his plans will not succeed or help him.

Daniel 11:17

Antiochus hopes that, since his daughter is queen of Egypt, she will eventually invite him to come and take over Egypt. But when Cleopatra marries Ptolemy Epiphanes (a descendant of Ptolemy Philopater) of Egypt, she falls in love with him. She stops paying attention to her father and has no desire to bring her father into Egypt as the king.

After this, he [Antiochus the Great] will turn back toward the fortresses of his own country but will stumble and fall, to be seen no more [he dies].

Daniel 11:19

Antiochus Epiphanes

Verses 21–35 deal with the exploits of Antiochus Epiphanes (175–104 B.C.). He is a significant individual and serves as a prototype of the Antichrist, who will dominate the world prior to the return of Jesus Christ. This passage can be divided into three sections: his rise to power, his battles, and his vengeance against Palestine.

His Rise to Power

He will be succeeded by a contemptible person who has not been given the honor of royalty [he didn't deserve to be king]. He will invade the kingdom when its people feel secure, and he will seize it through intrigue. Then an overwhelming army will be swept away before him; both it and a prince of the covenant [probably referring to the high priest Onian, who was executed by Antiochus] will be destroyed. After coming to an agreement with him, he will act deceitfully, and with only a few people he will rise to power. When the richest provinces feel secure, he will invade them and will achieve what neither his fathers nor his forefathers did. He will distribute plunder, loot and wealth among his followers. He will plot the overthrow of fortresses—but only for a time.

Daniel 11:21–24

There are two primary characteristics of Antiochus Epiphanes. First, he is a master of deceit. Second, he is a persecutor of the Jewish people.

His Battles

He defeats the king of the South (Egypt).

With a large army he will stir up his strength and courage against the king of the South.

Daniel 11:25

At a later time he confronts the Egyptians.

At the appointed time he will invade the South again [Egypt], but this time the outcome will be different from what it was before.

Daniel 11:29

The first time he defeats Egypt. The second time he does not. Why?

> Ships of the western coastlands [a reference to the rise of the Roman
> Empire] will oppose him, and he will lose heart.
>
> Daniel 11:30

History records that when Antiochus Epiphanes comes down to Egypt
for the second time, he is met by a Roman general (Popilus Laenus) in
the desert outside of Egypt. This Roman general delivers a letter to Antiochus Epiphanes from the Roman Senate. The letter basically says, "You
are forbidden from going to war against Egypt." Antiochus reads the letter. He vacillates. He is hesitant. He does not know what to do. The Roman
general approaches him, draws a circle in the sand around him, and says,
"You must answer to the Roman Senate before I will allow you to step
out of the circle." Antiochus agrees to withdraw. He loses heart and returns
home.

His Vengeance against Palestine

On the way back from Egypt, Antiochus goes through Palestine and
vents his frustration and anger on the Jewish people.

> Then he will turn back and vent his fury against the holy covenant [the
> people of Israel]. He will return and show favor [in Israel] to those who
> forsake the holy covenant.
>
> Daniel 11:30

Having been confronted by the power of Rome and forced to back down
with his army, he gets angry, and takes out his anger on Israel. The Jewish
record of this anger and fury is incredible.

> Then the king [Antiochus Epiphanes] issued a proclamation to his whole
> kingdom that all were to become a single people, each renouncing his par-
> ticular customs. All the pagans conformed to the king's decree, and many
> Israelites chose to accept his religion, sacrificing to idols and profaning
> the sabbath. The king also sent instructions by messenger to Jerusalem
> and the towns of Judah directing them to adopt customs foreign to the
> country, banning holocausts, sacrifices and libations from the sanctuary,
> profaning sabbaths and feasts, defiling the sanctuary and the sacred min-
> isters, building altars, precincts and shrines for idols, sacrificing pigs and
> unclean beasts, leaving their sons uncircumcised, and prostituting them-

selves to all kinds of impurity and abomination, so that they would forget the Law and revoke all observance of it. . . .

Many of the people—that is, every apostate from the Law—rallied to them, and so committed evil in the country, forcing Israel into hiding in all their places of refuge. On the fifteenth day of Chislev in the year one hundred and forty-five the king [Antiochus Epiphanes] erected the abomination of desolation above the altar. . . .

1 Maccabees 1:41–57 JB

Let me pause for just a moment. This abomination in the sanctuary brought about by Antiochus Epiphanes is predicted to recur just prior to the return of Christ. There were many in Israel who stood firm and found courage. They chose death rather than compromise. It was a dreadful wrath that visited Israel. Note the predictions made by Daniel several hundred years before it happened:

His armed forces will rise up to desecrate the temple fortress and will abolish the daily sacrifice. Then they will set up the abomination that causes desolation. With flattery he will corrupt those who have violated the covenant, but the people who know their God will firmly resist him.

Daniel 11:31–32

Insight

There is more to life than the acquisition of power and the accumulation of material things. When I read about all of these wars and all of the conflicts and the marching north and the marching south, I conclude, "There is more to life than getting power, and there is more to life than accumulating things." This may surprise you, but all of these guys are dead. Gone! When they died, their conquests and defeats came to an end. All of their military conquests. All of their accumulation of things. All of the elephants, infantry, and cavalry. All of the deceptive, manipulative schemes that they had planned. All of the gold vessels that they had accumulated. Gone! Over with! Unless you are a student of ancient history, you probably had not heard the names of any of them until you read this chapter.

The words of Jesus Christ can be written over Daniel chapter 11. "Do not store up for yourselves treasures on earth, where moth and rust destroy, and where thieves break in and steal. But store up for yourselves treasures in heaven" (Matt. 6:19–20).

Life is so brief. We devote our lives to accumulating things, to getting a bigger house, a bigger boat, and a bigger cottage at the lake. We devote our lives to getting a bigger office and more degrees. We devote our lives to expanding our business. We devote our lives to getting a better car and a better second car and a better third car. We spend our short period on this earth accumulating, getting, securing, getting power, getting things, getting cars, getting baggage, getting junk! And we don't realize that one day we are going to die and face God, and it won't amount to a hill of beans what car you drove or what kind of house you lived in or what kind of title you had on the door or how far up the corporate ladder you rose. The only thing that will matter is, "Did I live my life in this brief span of time for God?"

Prayer

Do not store up for yourselves treasures on earth, where moth and rust destroy, and where thieves break in and steal. But store up for yourselves treasures in heaven, where moth and rust do not destroy, and where thieves do not break in and steal. For where your treasure is, there will your heart be also.

Matthew 6:19–21

Dear Lord, remind me in the material world in which I live that my treasure must be in heaven. Help me to live today with heaven's perspective. With heaven's values. With heaven's hope. Let me deposit time, resources, and energy in the bank of heaven. Amen.

Chapter Sixteen

The Rise of Antichrist and Armageddon

Daniel 11:36–45

The last part of the eleventh chapter of Daniel (vv. 36–45) deals with the rise of the future Antichrist and the final battle of Armageddon. In examining these predictions, we want to explore other passages of Scripture that also deal with these issues. First, some preliminary questions about Antichrist that we have already discussed in our study of Daniel's prophecies.

The Origin of Antichrist

Where Does Antichrist Come From?

He gave me this explanation: "The fourth beast is a fourth kingdom that will appear on earth [actually the Roman Empire]. It will be different from all the other kingdoms and will devour the whole earth, trampling it down and crushing it."

Daniel 7:23

This is phase one. The Roman Empire will emerge. It will conquer the world. All forces that oppose it will be crushed. It will attain power over the entire earth.

The ten horns [that come out of this beast] are ten kings who will come
from this kingdom.

Daniel 7:24

Apparently, as we approach the end of the world there will be a coalition
of ten separate kingdoms that will actually be a revival or a renewal of the
ancient Roman Empire. Only this time, it's a federation of separate nations.

After them another king will arise [Antichrist], different from the earlier ones;
he will subdue three kings. [That is, he will conquer three of the ten in the
renewed Roman Empire.] He will speak against the Most High and oppress
his saints and try to change the set times and the laws. The saints will be
handed over to him for a time, times and half a time [or three and a half years].

Daniel 7:24–25

Where does Antichrist originate? At the end of time there will be a
renewal of the ancient Roman Empire—a political federation of ten
nations. Out of those nations the future world leader will come. He will
come to power by achieving a coalition composed of three of those nations
that will then ultimately lead to power and influence over the entire coalition. So we are relatively safe to assume that Antichrist will most likely
emerge out of Europe.

What Will Antichrist Do?

Antichrist will forge a peace treaty with Palestine. He will bring peace
to that part of the world. Three and a half years later, he will break the
treaty and persecute the Jews.

He will confirm a covenant [a treaty] with many for one "seven" [a seven-
year period]. In the middle of the "seven" [three and a half years into this
unique peace treaty] he will put an end to sacrifice and offering [referring
to the temple]. And on a wing of the temple he will set up an abomination
that causes desolation [he will desecrate the temple in Jerusalem], until
the end that is decreed is poured out on him.

Daniel 9:27

So Antichrist will rise to power out of a renewed Roman Empire. He
will form a coalition with three of those nations that will ultimately influ-

ence the entire ten-nation federation. He will be a brilliant politician and negotiator. He will achieve the impossible. He will forge a peace treaty between Israel and the surrounding Arab nations. Worship will be revived in Jerusalem. The whole world will turn to this Antichrist as the ultimate personification of peace. Three and a half years into the peace treaty, he will break it and bring persecution against the Jews.

The Deification of Antichrist

> The king will do as he pleases. He will exalt and magnify himself above every god and will say unheard-of things against the God of gods. He will be successful until the time of wrath is completed, for what has been determined must take place.
>
> Daniel 11:36

Antichrist will have great power. He will do as he pleases. He will try to change the natural and moral laws (see Dan. 7:25). He will succeed in whatever he does (see Dan. 8:24). He will exercise power over the entire world (see Rev. 13:7). He will then exalt himself above all gods, including the true God. In fact, he will declare himself to be God.

> He will oppose and will exalt himself over everything that is called God or is worshiped, so that he sets himself up in God's temple, proclaiming himself to be God.
>
> 2 Thessalonians 2:4

> The beast was given a mouth to utter proud words and blasphemies and to exercise his authority for forty-two months. He opened his mouth to blaspheme God, and to slander his name and his dwelling place and those who live in heaven.
>
> Revelation 13:5–6

> He will be successful until the time of wrath is completed, for what has been determined must take place.
>
> Daniel 11:36

The "time of wrath" is the great tribulation period. This is referred to in several other passages of Scripture.

How awful that day will be!
  None will be like it.
It will be a time of trouble for Jacob,
  but he will be saved out of it.
                                        Jeremiah 30:7

Because of the increase of wickedness, the love of most will grow cold.
                                        Matthew 24:12

His Disregard of Others

He will show no regard for the gods of his fathers or for the one desired
by women, nor will he regard any god, but will exalt himself above them
all.
                                        Daniel 11:37

The word *regard* is the Hebrew word *sin,* which means to respect or
regard with understanding. Three things are mentioned that Antichrist
will disregard (disrespect).

1. *The god of his fathers.* He will break tradition. He will have no
regard for history or any respect for the past. It is as if the world did not
exist before he came on the scene. He makes a complete severance with
tradition. Even the religion of the past is discarded.

2. *The one desired by women.* The Hebrew text literally says that he
has no regard for "the desire of woman." Now what does that mean?
There are really three options.

First, some people think it refers to the desire of Hebrew women. The
desire that, one day, God would choose one of them to give birth to the
Messiah. It is the inner desire of Hebrew women to give birth to the Messiah. Essentially, when Antichrist comes on the scene he has absolutely
no respect or regard for Messiah—the one desired by Hebrew women.

Second, some people think it refers to the desired qualities of women—
qualities such as mercy, kindness, gentleness, and love. Antichrist is so
severe, so harsh, so dictatorial that there is no room for mercy, kindness,
gentleness, and love in his heart. He disregards these qualities that were
associated with women in ancient culture.

Third, some people think it refers to having a desire for women. Loving women. It is a very natural thing for men to have affection for women
and women to have affection for men. But Antichrist, unlike most other

human beings, has no desire for women. He is not tempted by affection or attraction to women. This is the best of the three options. Natural human relations have no appeal for him.

3. *Any god.* Antichrist will be completely antireligious. He will not regard *any* god: Eastern gods, Western gods, Hindu gods, the Christian or Jewish God.

His Desire for Materialism

> Instead of them, he will honor a god of fortresses; a god unknown to his father he will honor with gold and silver, with precious stones and costly gifts.
>
> Daniel 11:38

He will honor a god of "fortresses." This word is used six times in the Book of Daniel. In fact, it is used two other times in chapter 11 (vv. 7, 10). It refers to a place of military power and strength. Antichrist will not respect religion. Rather, he will respect military power (the god of fortresses). He will use his wealth to worship this god of military power. This means that he will invest great resources in building military strength.

His Dogma of Militarism

Antichrist dogma will be reduced to one word—POWER.

> He will attack the mightiest fortresses [the greatest centers of military power] with the help of a foreign god [probably the god of military might and armies] and will greatly honor those who acknowledge him [who form a coalition with him]. He will make them rulers over many people and will distribute the land at a price [a new world order with a reordering of society, powers, and nations].
>
> Daniel 11:39

He will overcome all other powers and eventually rule the world.

> Men worshiped the dragon because he had given authority to the beast, and they also worshiped the beast and asked, "Who is like the beast? Who can make war against him?"
>
> Revelation 13:4

The Mother of All Battles: Armageddon

Webster defines the word *Armageddon* as "the site or time of final and conclusive battle between the forces of good and evil." This is precisely what Daniel and other writers predict will happen at the end of time. Before examining the details of this battle as described in Daniel, let us look at John's description of this same battle as given in Revelation 16:12–16.

> The sixth angel poured out his bowl on the great river Euphrates, and its water was dried up to prepare the way for the kings from the East.
>
> Revelation 16:12

The word *east* refers to kings who come from the land of the rising sun. It can refer to India, China, Japan, or the Orient in general.

As the world is prepared for this final battle of Armageddon, several things begin to happen. First, the entire Euphrates River is dried up. (One interesting side note: Recently there were threats from Turkey that they would close off the dam that ultimately allows the Euphrates River to flow. It is not beyond comprehension that one day this great river that flows through Iraq could be dried up.) The reason it is dried up is so that eastern armies can march with great swiftness from the east all the way to Palestine, where the battle is fought. One of the problems at the present moment is the limited number of bridges across the Euphrates River. During the Gulf War, one of the primary targets of the allied forces was the bridges over the Euphrates. Step number one, whether by natural or supernatural means, the Euphrates River is dried up. It is no longer an obstacle to advancing armies from the east.

The second event will be an increase of demonic activity.

> Then I saw three evil spirits that looked like frogs; they came out of the mouth of the dragon [probably Satan], out of the mouth of the beast [Antichrist] and out of the mouth of the false prophet [the one who symbolizes one world religion]. They are spirits of demons performing miraculous signs, and they go out to the kings of the whole world [this final conflict encompasses all of the military powers of the world], to gather them for the battle on the great day of God Almighty.
>
> Revelation 16:13–14

This is war! There are two Greek words used for *battle*. One is an individual battle or a single conflict. The other is a broader term that means *war* and could mean many individual battles. This second word is used here. Armageddon is probably not a single battle. There will be a final battle when Jesus comes and defeats the forces of evil, but Armageddon is more likely a war of individual battles waged over a specific period of time.

The third event is the coming of Jesus Christ.

> Behold, I come like a thief! Blessed is he who stays awake and keeps his clothes with him, so that he may not go naked and be shamefully exposed.
>
> Revelation 16:15

The fourth event is the battle of Armageddon.

> Then they [the demons that had been let loose] gathered the kings together [the military powers of the world] to the place that in Hebrew is called Armageddon [or Mount Megiddo, in the northern part of Israel adjacent to the valley of Esralon].
>
> Revelation 16:16

The battle will take place beyond this valley. It will occur along a two-hundred-mile front (see Rev. 14:20). Daniel fills in more of the details in his predictions.

The Setting of the Stage

> At the time of the end . . .
> Daniel 11:40

In our study of Daniel, we have already established several events that will happen during the endtimes. Toward the end of time, there will be a revival of the ancient alliance of the Roman Empire—a political and economic cooperation between ten countries. Out of the political base, a world leader will emerge. He is called the Antichrist. He will come to power primarily through brilliant diplomatic initiatives. For example, he will solve one of the most perplexing problems in our world today—the Jewish-Arab conflict. Because of his incredible, brilliant diplomatic skills, he will forge an alliance (a peace treaty) with Israel and the Arab nations. This peace treaty will usher in a new world order. It will bring security and peace to the Middle East. Because of those brilliant diplomatic skills, he will be proclaimed as a new world hero. Attention will be paid to one-world government. We will live interdependent with each other. A one-world religion will emerge. Then during this period of unparalleled peace, something happens to interrupt the peace. What happens occurs during two phases.

Phase 1: Consolidation of Power

> At the time of the end the king of the South will engage him [Antichrist] in battle, and the king of the North [Syria and beyond] will storm out against him [against Antichrist] with chariots and cavalry and a great fleet of ships. He will invade many countries [he will defeat this northern/southern coalition] and sweep through them like a flood. He will also invade the Beautiful Land [Palestine]. Many countries will fall, but Edom, Moab [southeast of Palestine, perhaps modern-day Jordan] and the leaders of Ammon will be delivered from his hand.
>
> Daniel 11:40–41

Antichrist comes to power and forges a peace treaty with Israel. Then a coalition of Egypt, Syria, and perhaps others decide to fight Israel. Antichrist has already forged a peace treaty guaranteeing the security of Israel, and so to repel the threat against Israel, Antichrist goes to war against this coalition. Further details about these events are given in Ezekiel 38–39.

> After many days you will be called to arms. In future years you will invade a land that has recovered from war, whose people were gathered from many nations to the mountains of Israel, which had long been desolate. They had been brought out from the nations, and now all of them live in safety.
>
> Ezekiel 38:8

Two factors of importance are identified in this verse. First, the people of Israel have been gathered back to the land of Palestine. Second, they are living in security and safety. When these two events are true, the stage is set for the endtimes.

> The word of the LORD came to me: "Son of man, set your face against God, of the land of Magog, the chief prince of Meshech and Tubal; proph-

esy against him and say: 'This is what the Sovereign LORD says: I am against you, O Gog, chief prince of Meshech and Tubal. I will turn you around, put hooks in your jaws and bring you out with your whole army— your horses, your horsemen fully armed, and a great horde with large and small shields, all of them brandishing their swords. Persia [modern-day Iran], Cush [either Ethiopia or Sudan] and Put [Libya] will be with them, all with shields and helmets, also Gomer with all its troops, and Beth Togarmah [Turkey] from the far north with all its troops—the many nations with you.'"

Ezekiel 38:1–6

This suggests a coalition of northern peoples along with Egyptians and North Africans. This coalition forms to do battle with Israel. Who are these people? There are at least two options.

1. *A Russian-Arab Coalition.* For many years this was the most popular interpretation of this coalition. Some people think that the land of Magog refers to the city of Moscow. In addition, the words *chief prince* come from the Hebrew word *Rosh* which sounds like Russia.

2. *Holy Jihad.* The second option is that this coalition refers to a holy jihad of Arab and Muslim peoples. The people mentioned from the north may be people in the southern part of the old Soviet Union in the Armenian highlands. There are Muslim peoples who would share the same religion as many of the Arab nations. We know that during the time of Antichrist, temple worship is restored in Jerusalem. This site of the temple is also one of the most sacred of Muslim sites—the Dome of the Rock. Perhaps the restoration of Jewish worship at this site will so anger the Muslims that they will forge a holy jihad to attack Israel.

According to Daniel, Antichrist will defeat this coalition (whether it is a Russian-Arab or holy jihad coalition).

He will extend his power over many countries; Egypt will not escape. He will gain control of the treasures of gold and silver and all the riches of Egypt, with the Libyans and Nubians in submission.

Daniel 11:42–43

Phase 2: The Rebellion against Antichrist

But reports from the east and the north will alarm him, and he will set out in a great rage to destroy and annihilate many.

Daniel 11:44

The details of this disturbing news are given in the Book of Revelation (see Rev. 9:16; 16:12). This army from the east will be two million strong.

> He will pitch his royal tents between the seas at the beautiful holy mountain. Yet he will come to his end, and no one will help him.
>
> Daniel 11:45

It appears that Antichrist will initially oppose the advancing eastern army. Then Christ will return with his army, and all the armies (including the army of Antichrist) will turn against Jesus Christ.

While not all the details of the battle of Armageddon are given, there are several important details which are given.

1. *Political powers will be involved.* This includes:

the North—Russia
the South—Egypt and Arab coalition
the East—the Orient
Europe—the revived Roman Empire

2. *The Middle East will be the center of the conflict.* The nation of Israel will be the center stage where this battle is fought.

3. *There will be great destruction and loss of human life.*

Insight

1. *Is the world being prepared for Antichrist?* I have phrased this insight in the form of a question. Are we living in the last days? Is the world being prepared to accept Antichrist? We know that when Antichrist arrives, he will proclaim himself to be God, he will advocate materialism, and he will solve the problems of the world through military strength. Whether or not we are in the endtimes is open for debate. But one thing is sure, the world is militarily ready and spiritually open to a person like Antichrist.

Antichrist will influence the world with superior military power. He will solve the problems of the world with weapons. Could it be that the nuclear arsenal of this world awaits use by the Antichrist?

As well as having the military potential, most of the world is ready for the deification of Antichrist.

> The king will do as he pleases. He will exalt and magnify himself above every god and will say unheard-of things against the God of gods. He will be successful until the time of wrath is completed, for what has been determined must take place.
>
> Daniel 11:36

Is it reasonable to assume that a sophisticated and educated world would accept a person who claims to be God? On the surface, this would seem foolish. But it is not as far-fetched as it would seem.

There is intellectual acceptance of the idea of humans being god. Philosophical humanism is a system that essentially deifies human beings. It was developed by the pre-Socratic philosopher Protaguras, who coined a phrase "man the measure." Man is the center of the universe. Man is the measure of all things. He is the one who establishes morals and values. God really is not the center of the universe—man is the center. The logical conclusion is that God is unnecessary, if he even exists at all. As human beings, we are the center of human history. We are the center of the universe. We are the ones who determine morality and values. We are the measure of all things.

Humanism is the underlying intellectual foundation of what we would call modern thinking, the scientific age, the age of empiricism, the age of rationalism. Humanism is a philosophy or attitude that addresses itself exclusively to the human as opposed to the divine or the supernatural, often accompanied by a belief that man is capable of reaching self-fulfillment without divine aid. I am the ultimate norm. I am the ultimate standard. I am the ultimate measure. If progress is to be made in the world in which we live, we sure can't depend on God! We must educate people. We must better society. We must influence people in a positive moral way. We really don't need God. All we need is ourselves, science, our own abilities, and our creativity. God is absolutely unnecessary.

Now I have oversimplified the philosophical implications of humanism, but the bottom line is, man is the measure, God is unnecessary. Could it be that the Antichrist is the ultimate expression and the highest ideal of humanistic philosophy? A person possessed of such incredible intellectual ability, a person possessed with a brilliant scientific mind, a person who is the ultimate expression of everything that is good about humanity and who offers to the world peace without God? In the words of John Lennon's song, "A world without a religion too." We don't need God. We don't need religion. All we need is ourselves.

New Age religion. New Age mania is sweeping the Western world. It is built on the basic ideas of Eastern religion. Its roots are in pantheism. Pantheism teaches that "all is God, God is all." I am god. You are god. We are all god. God is the tree. God is the bird. New Age religion is the journey to discover the god who is within us. Could it be that Antichrist will be the guru of New Age thinking? The ultimate experience of God?

When I think of the predominate grip of humanism, secularism, and philosophical materialism in the society in which we live, it is not hard for me to stretch my mind to a point and time in human history when someone comes on the stage of history possessed with brilliant negotiating and diplomatic skills. Someone with an incredible education and background. Someone who declares, "The problem with the world is God. It is Jew and Arab. It is Muslim and Christian. It is Catholic and Protestant. The problem of the world is God. We don't need God. We only need our own ability. After all, we are god. We are the measure of all things. We're the ones who determine our fate and our future." And the world turns to this incredible individual and says, "You know, you're right. We are somebody. We possess the ability to alter society forever. We can bring peace into the world." Turning from organized religion, the world proclaims this individual as the ultimate savior of humanity.

2. *God is in control.* The events predicted for the end of the world are filled with doom and gloom. But remember, God is in control, and all of history is moving toward the coming of Jesus Christ in glory and power. Are we living in the terminal generation? Frankly, I don't know. It does appear to me, however, that the pieces of human history are being put together. Israel is back in the land. Europe has joined together in an economic community. We are working for a new world order in the Middle East. With the injustices in South Africa, the injustices against the Palestinians, the problems in Northern Ireland, the problems in El Salvador and Nicaragua and around the world, the stage of human history is set for a superhuman being who, with diplomatic ingenuity and military might, can bring world peace. When he does, "Watch out," Jesus says, "it's the beginning of the time of Jacob's trouble." Whether Christ comes soon or tarries thousands of years, one thing is for sure—God is in control!

Prayer

Lord, the times in which we live are complex and dark. The world is filled with war, hatred, poverty, abuse, injustice, and racism. In fact, the list of sins is endless. At times it seems that the world is mad and out of control. I praise you that you are still on the throne of the universe. You are not surprised. Thank you for the assurance that you are the God of history and eternity. Amen.

Chapter Seventeen

The Great Tribulation

Daniel 12:1–13

> At that time Michael, the great prince who protects your people, will arise. There will be a time of distress such as has not happened from the beginning of nations until then. But at that time your people—everyone whose name is found written in the book—will be delivered. Multitudes who sleep in the dust of the earth will awake: some to everlasting life, others to shame and everlasting contempt.
>
> Daniel 12:1–2

A Time of Distress

At the end of time there will be a "time of distress such as has not happened from the beginning of nations until then" (v. 1). God is telling Daniel that at the end of time something significant is going to happen. There will be a specific period of time in the last days of significant distress. In fact, of such distress and oppression that it will be unparalleled in the course of human history. There never has been nor will there ever be a period of time with such significant distress as this period of time. We call it the great tribulation. As you study the Scriptures, you will find remarkable consistency from the early chapters of the Old Testament to the final chapters of the New Testament in regard to this event. It is called, "the day of the Lord" (Amos 5:18–20), "that day" (Zech.

14:6), "the day," and "the great day" (Rev. 6:17). We want to look at a number of passages that describe this day before we examine the last chapter of the Book of Daniel. As we consider these passages, we want to ask several questions:

- When will this time of distress occur?
- Who is involved with this distress?
- Why does it happen?
- What will it be like?

The Tribulation Predicted in the Old Testament

1. Deuteronomy 4:30–31

When you are in distress and all these things have happened to you, then in later days you will return to the LORD your God and obey him. For the LORD your God is a merciful God; he will not abandon or destroy you or forget the covenant with your forefathers, which he confirmed to them by oath.

When? The last days.
Who? The nation of Israel will be restored to the land.

2. Jeremiah 30:7

How awful that day will be!
    None will be like it.
It will be a time of trouble for Jacob,
    but he will be saved out of it.

What will it be like? An awful day, a time of trouble.
Who? Jacob.
Why? God will deliver his people.

3. Joel 2:1–2

Blow the trumpet in Zion;
    sound the alarm on my holy hill.
Let all who live in the land tremble,
    for the day of the LORD is coming.

It is close at hand—
    a day of darkness and gloom,
    a day of clouds and blackness.
Like dawn spreading across the
       mountains
    a large and mighty army comes,
such as never was of old
    nor ever will be in ages to come.

Who? Zion.

What will it be like? Darkness, gloom, clouds, blackness. A large and mighty army.

4. *Zephaniah 1:14–15*

The great day of the LORD is
       near—
    near and coming quickly.
Listen! The cry on the day of the
       LORD will be bitter,
    the shouting of the warrior
       there.
That day will be a day of wrath,
    a day of distress and anguish,
a day of trouble and ruin,
    a day of darkness and gloom,
    a day of clouds and blackness.

What will it be like? A day of wrath, distress, anguish, trouble, ruin, darkness, gloom, clouds, and blackness.

Why? The whole world is judged (see Zeph. 1:18).

Let me summarize the teaching of the Old Testament in regard to the tribulation.

- When will it happen? At the end of time.
- Who will be involved? Israel and the world.
- What will it be like? A day of trouble and distress.
- Why does it happen? God will judge the world and save Israel.

The Tribulation Predicted in the New Testament

1. *Matthew 24:15–21*

So when you see standing in the holy place "the abomination that causes desolation," spoken of through the prophet Daniel—let the reader understand—
then let those who are in Judea flee to the mountains. Let no one on the roof
of his house go down to take anything out of the house. Let no one in the
field go back to get his cloak. How dreadful it will be in those days for preg-
nant women and nursing mothers! Pray that your flight will not take place in
winter or on the Sabbath. For then there will be great distress, unequaled
from the beginning of the world until now—and never to be equaled again.

When? At the end of the age (see Matt. 24:3).
Who? Antichrist and Israel.
What? Great distress.

2. *Luke 21:25–26*

There will be signs in the sun, moon and stars. On the earth, nations will
be in anguish and perplexity at the roaring and tossing of the sea. Men
will faint from terror, apprehensive of what is coming on the world, for
the heavenly bodies will be shaken.

Who? All nations.
What? Cataclysmic events in the solar system.

3. *Revelation 6:15–17*

Then the kings of the earth, the princes, the generals, the rich, the mighty,
and every slave and every free man hid in caves and among the rocks of
the mountains. They called to the mountains and the rocks, "Fall on us and
hide us from the face of him who sits on the throne and from the wrath of
the Lamb! For the great day of their wrath has come, and who can stand?"

Why? A day of wrath and judgment.
Who? The whole world.

Let me summarize the teachings of the Old Testament and the New
Testament on the topic of the tribulation.

- When will it happen? At the end of time.
- Who will be involved? Israel and the whole world.
- What will it be like? The greatest distress the world has ever seen.
- Why will it happen? God will use the tribulation to judge the ungodly in the world and to restore Israel to faith by delivering them.

Where Is the Church during the Tribulation?

None of the passages that refer to the tribulation mention the church. Where's the church? We read about Jacob. We read about Judea. We read about Palestine. We read about the world. We read about the nations. We read about God restoring his covenant to Israel. All of this happens during this time of judgment on planet earth that ultimately culminates with the coming of Jesus Christ. But where is the church? *Unmentioned* in every passage dealing with the tribulation.

There are three interpretations. One, the church really is there on planet earth. It goes through this time of trouble, but it is not mentioned by name. Two, Israel and the church are essentially the same thing. These are the people of God—when it talks about the descendants of Jacob, it spiritually includes the church. Therefore, when God promises Israel salvation and restoration, that promise finds its fulfillment, not in a literal Israel, but in the church. Three, the reason the church is not mentioned is that it's not there. It is not in existence on planet earth during this period of time called the great day of God's wrath. Let us consider these options.

1. *It is there but not mentioned by name*. I could accept this option if we were only talking about the Old Testament. We know for sure that the church was a mystery in the Old Testament (see Eph. 3:1–6). It was not understood. It was not comprehended. It was not revealed. The church is a mystery that was revealed in the New Testament. So all of the prophecies in the Old Testament that deal with the tribulation would not mention the church. Why? Because the church was a mystery in the Old Testament.

But what about the New Testament? Why is the church not mentioned in these passages about the tribulation? After all, the tribulation is mentioned by Jesus, Paul, and John. There are many passages that deal with this day of distress. Is the church there but not mentioned? Let me suggest that it is highly unlikely. Why? Because the central message of the entire New Testament is the church. It is not Israel. It is not Jerusalem. It is not Palestine. The central focus of the Gospels, the Book of Acts, the Epistles, and even the Book of the Revelation is God's work through the church—not Israel. If the church is the central focus of the entire New Testament, it would be strange indeed to speak of this prophetic theme and not even mention the church, which is the central theme of God's program.

2. *Israel and the church are the same*. This interpretation sees Israel and the church as synonymous. All the predictions about Israel and the tribulation are actually fulfilled through the church, which is spiritual Israel. Can Israel and the church be considered as the same entity, or does God treat them as specific entities? I believe that they are separate entities, and Bible prophecy must be interpreted with this in mind. Consider the following passages:

> They [Israel] will fall by the sword and will be taken as prisoners to all nations. [Israel will be dispersed into the entire world.] Jerusalem will be trampled on [overcome, dominated] by the Gentiles until the times of the Gentiles are fulfilled.
>
> Luke 21:24

Christ introduces a concept that in the working of God here on planet earth there is a period of time called the time of the Gentiles. During that period of time, Israel will be dispersed among all the nations of the world. The Gentiles will dominate Jerusalem, but the times of the Gentiles will come to an end. Paul amplifies on this concept in Romans.

> I do not want you to be ignorant of this mystery, brothers, so that you may not be conceited: Israel has experienced a hardening in part [hardening of the heart, a resistance to God] until the full number of the Gentiles has come in [into the Kingdom].
>
> Romans 11:25

The nation of Israel is now resisting the working of God because God is involved in a program of calling Gentiles to himself. One day he will be finished with that program. All of the Gentiles will be called in. Then notice what happens:

> And so [or after that] all Israel will be saved, as it is written:

"The deliverer will come from Zion;
    he will turn godlessness away
        from Jacob.
And this is my covenant with them
    when I take away their sins."
                                        Romans 11:26–27

Let me try to summarize all of this very simply. Jesus said Israel will be dispersed all over the world. The Gentiles will dominate Jerusalem until the time of the Gentiles is completed. Paul says that right now Israel resists the working of God. God is at work among the Gentiles calling out a people. One day, God will be finished calling together the church. He will then return to Israel. In that day, after the time of the Gentiles is completed, God will save all of Israel at once. The point is this: Israel and the church are not synonymous terms. Even a casual reading of the Scripture causes us to conclude that Israel is dispersed. God is calling out a church—a people from the Gentiles all over the world. When that is completed, God will then fulfill his promise that he will save Israel (v. 26). Why? Because the covenant of God cannot and will not be changed.

All of the promises of God in the Old Testament one day will be literally fulfilled, because the election and calling of God is irrevocable. Therefore, Israel and the church are not the same thing. Consequently, one cannot assume that the predictions of the tribulation for Israel are actually fulfilled in the church. Israel and the church are separate entities. The prediction for Israel must be fulfilled in Israel. The predictions for the church must be fulfilled in the church.

3. *The church does not go through the tribulation.* I believe that the most plausible explanation for the absence of the church during the events of the tribulation period is that God removed the church from planet earth. In fact, Christ made such a promise (see Rev. 3:10). So what happens to the church? It is taken out of the world. We call it the rapture.

Brothers, we do not want you to be ignorant about those who fall asleep, or to grieve like the rest of men, who have no hope. We believe that Jesus died and rose again and so we believe that God will bring with Jesus those who have fallen asleep in him. According to the Lord's own word, we tell you that we who are still alive, who are left till the coming of the Lord, will certainly not precede those who have fallen asleep. For the Lord himself will come down from heaven, with a loud command, with the voice of the archangel and with the trumpet call of God, and the dead in Christ will rise first. After that, we who are still alive and are left will be caught up together with them in the clouds to meet the Lord in the air. And so we will be with the Lord forever. Therefore encourage each other with these words.

1 Thessalonians 4:13–18

The coming of the Lord occurs in two phases. First, he comes *for* the saints. Second, after the great tribulation, he comes *with* the angels and the saints (see 2 Thess. 1:7–8; Rev. 19:17–21).

The Deliverance of Israel

At that time Michael, the great prince who protects your people, will arise. There will be a time of distress such as has not happened from the beginning of nations until then. But at that time your people—everyone whose name is found written in the book—will be delivered.

Daniel 12:1

God will come to deliver his people (the Jews). It will be those whose names are written in the book. What kind of book is this? When a Jewish child was born, the name of that child was entered into a genealogical record. It was very important to understand and keep a record of one's roots. Later on when the synagogue came into existence, the synagogue provided this service. After the birth, they would enter the name of that person into the record of the synagogue—into the book. It identified that person with the covenant. It identified that person with God's people.

The idea here is that there is another book of far greater significance than the genealogical human record. In other passages of the Bible it is called the book of life. It is God, not a human being, who enters one's name into the book. The names of those who are placed in the book are those who have turned to God. At the end of this time of distress, Israel is delivered. But not all of Israel, only those who have turned in faith to God. During the tribulation, people will turn to God. When they do, their names will be written in the book of life.

All inhabitants of the earth will worship the beast—all whose names have not been written in the book of life belonging to the Lamb that was slain from the creation of the world.

Revelation 13:8

The Resurrection of the Dead

Multitudes who sleep in the dust of the earth will awake: some to everlasting life, others to shame and everlasting contempt. Those who are wise
will shine like the brightness of the heavens, and those who lead many to
righteousness, like the stars for ever and ever.

Daniel 12:2–3

Death is described in these verses as those "who sleep in the dust of
the earth." Resurrection is described as awakening. Some have used
these verses to advocate the idea of soul sleep. In other words, at death
the soul goes into a coma or unconscious state. Several times in the
Scriptures, death is referred to as sleep (see Matt. 9:24; 1 Cor. 15:51;
1 Thess. 4:13). However, this does *not* mean that the soul is asleep. The
Bible makes it clear that at death the soul separates from the body and
exists in a state of conscious bliss or conscious suffering (see Luke
16:19–31; Luke 23:43; 2 Cor. 5:8; Phil. 1:23). The imagery of sleep is
used to describe the condition of the body, not the soul. The body returns
to dust. It no longer lives and moves. But one day it will be resurrected
(see Dan. 12:2). This text in Daniel identifies two separate eternal des-
tinies: heaven and hell.

How Long Will It Be?

Then I, Daniel, looked, and there before me stood two others, one on this
bank of the river and one on the opposite bank. One of them said to the
man clothed in linen, who was above the water of the river, "How long
will it be before these astonishing things are fulfilled?"

The man clothed in linen, who was above the waters of the river, lifted
his right hand and his left hand toward heaven, and I heard him swear by
him who lives forever, saying, "It will be for a time, times and half a time.
When the power of the holy people has been finally broken, all these things
will be completed. . . .

"From the time that the daily sacrifice is abolished and the abomination that causes desolation is set up, there will be 1,290 days."

Daniel 12:5–7, 11

The final question is one that deals with time. One of the persons on
the banks of the river asks the man clothed in linen (perhaps Jesus

Christ), "How long will it be before these astonishing things are fulfilled?" (v. 6). His answer is "a time, times and half a time" (v. 7). We
have dealt with this time span before (see Dan. 4:16, 23, 32, 34). It is
a span of three and one-half years. This period of time is further identified in verse 11.

> From the time that the daily sacrifice is abolished and the abomination
> that causes desolation is set up, there will be 1,290 days.

Insight

> As for you, go your way till the end. You will rest, and then at the end of
> the days you will rise to receive your allotted inheritance.
>
> Daniel 12:13

In light of all of these incredible events, how should we respond? The
closing verse of the Book of Daniel offers a threefold admonition. Whatever your interpretation of these prophecies, we would do well to heed
this last verse.

1. *Go your way till the end.* Some people get all absorbed and consumed with endtime prophecies. They speculate. They identify people.
They even set dates. God's advice to Daniel is great. "Go your way."
Don't be submerged in the world of Bible prophecy. Keep on loving
and serving God. God has given us something to do until the end of
the age.

> Then Jesus came to them and said, "All authority in heaven and earth has
> been given to me. Therefore go and make disciples of all nations, baptiz-
> ing them in the name of the Father and of the Son and of the Holy Spirit,
> and teaching them to obey everything I have commanded you. And surely
> I am with you always, to the very end of the age."
>
> Matthew 28:18–20

2. *You will rest.* Our hope is not in the political systems of this world.
Our hope is in eternity. One day we will enter into that rest. All the struggles and trials will be worth it.

3. *You will rise to receive your allotted inheritance.* Our reward is in
heaven. We have the promise of heaven and that reward.

I consider that our present sufferings are not worth comparing with the glory that will be revealed in us.

Romans 8:18

Prayer

Lord, when the world around me seems to be in turmoil, help me to keep on serving and loving you. I know that one day I will enter your rest and receive my reward. Until then, keep me serving and loving you. Amen.